Precious In The Sight Of God

by Lea Fowler

QUALITY PUBLICATIONS
P.O. BOX 1060
ABILENE, TEXAS 79604

© Lea Fowler 1983

0-89137-428-0

Contents

Chapter 1. Mother Eve 7
Chapter 2. The Princess 17
Chapter 3. The Egyptian Concubine 25
Chapter 4. God Loves Babies 31
Chapter 5. God Loves Unborn Babies.................... 35
Chapter 6. The Unloved Wife 39
Chapter 7. Saved From A Jealous Rival 47
Chapter 8. The Fool's Wife.......................... 51
Chapter 9. The Indiscreet Bather 59
Chapter 10. Widows 65
Chapter 11. The Depressed Woman 73
Chapter 12. The Carpenter's Wife 81
Chapter 13. The Samaritan Woman 91
Chapter 14. The Frustrated Cook 97
Chapter 15. God's Bad Girls 103
Chapter 16. The Ten-Talent Woman 115
Chapter 17. The Single Woman 121
Chapter 18. Who's Boss? 127
Chapter 19. Whom God Has Joined Together 137
Chapter 20. The Two Shall Become One 143

Dedicated To:

My holy Father as a small token of love for His great love and goodness and understanding.

Foreword

When I search my heart I find that my dearest longing is to be "precious in His sight." Could this ever be, someone like me?

Gratitude

To my loving husband, Russ, who believed in the book more than I did.

To my sister-in-Him, Sherry Pierce, who labored in typing, grammar, and punctuation.

To my son, Tom, and two daughters, Judy and Becky, who encouraged me from the heart.

To Fran, who fasted and prayed for this effort.

To Ruth, who listened weekly to the new chapters.

To the many sisters who read with correcting pencil in hand and believed in it.

To the New England Christians who kept prodding me to finish it so they could have a copy. Finally, here it is!

Introduction

As I read His book I am constantly touched by the tenderness of the Father and the Son with womankind. God deals with us "according to knowledge." He sets the perfect example to godly men who are made in His image, how to love their wives who are fashioned by the hands of God. It is my hope to show women in these troubled times God's concern for us and how near He is to His daughters and His potential daughters. If some of these chapters send you hurrying to the Book, I will be happy!

Note:
All biblical quotations are taken from the New American Standard Version unless otherwise noted.

Precious We'd Like To Be

If we could live with our lights trimmed bright,
We'd turn out to be like gold in His sight.
Like Sarah we'd grow as the years fly by,
Dying to self—learning to die.

A quiet gentle spirit, such a prize to seek.
It's an acquired virtue, not for the weak.
It takes prayer and time and exercise mental,
To want to be quiet or choose to be gentle.

To stress inward beauty and soft peddle the looks,
Is to go against nature, T.V., and books,
But it *should* end up perfect, it *would* end up right,
For we *could* end up precious, like gold in His sight.

Lea Fowler
Based on 1 Peter 3

Chapter 1

MOTHER EVE

"Now the man called his wife's name Eve, because she was the mother of all the living" (Genesis 3:20).

Should we not start our study with Mother Eve, for in her we have our roots? Won't it be wonderful to meet her someday? And yet, Eve is so often maligned and misunderstood by people who should know better, even Bible students.

How often have you heard, "Because of Eve you are supposed to keep your mouth shut; I'm the boss and I'm not interested in anything you have to say!" Or, "If it hadn't been for Eve, women would have equal rights. She ruined it all for us." These people forget that God forgave. They forget Eve did not sin willfully, but was greatly deceived. She was naive. She believed a lie. She was shot down by her first enemy. The same enemy shoots us down daily, and often not because of naivete like Eve's but deliberate sin like Adam's.

Let us go back and re-study the beginning... the fall, the price that was paid, and how it affects us today.

This is the book of the generations of Adam. In the day when God created man, He made him in the likeness of God. He created them male and female, and He blessed them and named them Man in the day when they were created.

(Genesis 5:1,2)

Let Us make man in Our image, according to Our likeness; and let them rule over fish...birds...cattle...And

7

God created man in His own image, in the image of God He created him; male and female He created them...Be fruitful and multiply, and fill the earth, and subdue it...

(Genesis 1:26-28)

Mankind was made in the image of God, male and female. They were made in the image of the God-head. Mankind is a two-fold being, flesh and spirit. The flesh dies and corrupts, but the spirit returns to God who gave it. "Then the dust will return to God who gave it" (Ecclesiastes 12:7).

God made women with the same kind of spirit as men. She, too, was made to serve God and to feel the many frustrations and joys of being the created. There are many similarities in mankind, whether male or female. We share many of the same ambitions, hurts, disappointments, triumphs, and tragedies.

Adam was made first. God does all things well and "in decency and order." He made the stronger first, the protector. Adam was alone, as God wanted him to feel lonely. "It is not good for man to be alone; I will make him a helper suitable for him" (Genesis 2:18). I'll make him a helper who supplies anything that is lacking in him, one who fulfills his every need, one who completes him. I made *him*. I know his strengths and weaknesses, and I know what it takes to make him happy.

So God brought all of the animals and the birds to Adam to be named. As Adam named them, he saw that there was always the male and the female. The females were the "mothers" for the propagation of the species and the males were the "fathers" for the same purpose. The male was usually the stronger, the aggressive, and the female was the more docile.

But for Adam there was no helper, no one to be defended and protected, no one to comfort him and no one to love. God gave him Eve. Do we think that Eve was an afterthought? God slipped up? Or could it be that God was preparing Adam for Eve?

Man still needs to live long enough before he marries to know loneliness. When a man marries too young it is hard for him to be kind to a wife, to take the lead, to not misuse his strength, and to really appreciate the woman given to his care. The young tend to seek their own way, male and female.

God made the stronger first and then, in His divine wisdom, He made the weaker, the one who would always need to be encircled. The word husband means the "house-binder", the encircler. The

8

children were made next. Just as God made the grass before He made the beast, so He made man, then woman, and then child.

"And Adam said, 'This at last is the bone of my bones and flesh of my flesh'" (Genesis 2:23). His thoughts probably went like this. What has been lacking is now supplied. She was taken out of me and I am conscious of the loss. "So the Lord God caused a deep sleep to fall upon the man, and he slept; then He took one of his ribs, and closed up the flesh at that place. And the Lord God fashioned into a woman the rib which He had taken from the man, and brought her to the man" (Genesis 2:21,22). Think about that! The Lord God fashioned the woman with His own hands. He shaped her; He made her suitable for her husband. He made her smaller, softer, prettier, more curious, more affectionate, playful, and more naive.

Wouldn't you love to have seen Eve? Just imagine her beauty! Wouldn't you love to have seen Adam's face when he saw this woman, fashioned by the hands of God! What a happy day that wedding day. And in what a wonderful place to spend your honeymoon! Eden.

"And the man said, 'This is it'" (Genesis 2:23). How every bride wishes her husband could continue to feel this same excitement and pleasure at her presence. God wishes the same thing; He tells us so.

> Drink water from your own cistern, and fresh water from your own well.
> Should your springs be dispersed abroad, streams of water in the streets?
> Let them be yours alone, and not for strangers with you.
> Let your fountain be blessed, and rejoice in the wife of your youth.
> As a loving hind and a graceful doe, let her breasts satisfy you at all times;
> Be exhilarated (ravished) always with her love.
> For why should you, my son, be exhilarated with an adulteress, and embrace the bosom of a foreigner?
> For the ways of a man are before the eyes of the Lord, and he watches all his paths (Proverbs 5:15-21).

Note how God teaches His men to prolong the honeymoon for as long as he lives. He instructs the man to rejoice in his marriage. Have fun. Make love, and don't look at another woman. Make a covenant with your eyes as did Job to not even look at the younger woman as your wife grows older.

9

A leading woman's magazine made a survey of marriages and sexual relations and found, probably to their surprise, that religious women make the best wives. This *should* be so, for they ought to be the most loving, the most available, and have the greatest desire to please their husbands. They should marry for life, "forsaking all others till death do us part."

"Enjoy life with the woman whom you love all the days of your fleeting life which He has given you under the sun; for this is your reward in life, and in your toil in which you have labored under the sun" (Ecclesiastes 9:9).

God did not give Adam a child for a companion. Children are wonderful, exciting, and fill a very needed place in our lives, but they cannot supply what is lacking in man. God did not make another man for Adam. Another man would have removed some of the loneliness, but would still not have been able to supply all the needs. Woman's very femininity, her perceptions and her tenderness are desirable qualities to a man. We know that *whatever* was lacking in Adam was supplied by Eve, for *God* made a helper suitable for him.

"And the man and his wife were both naked and were not ashamed" (Genesis 2:45). Before sin came there was lovemaking in all its beauty and no shame. Adam and Eve were two young adults living in Paradise. They were commanded to be fruitful and multiply just as all of God's other creatures were so commanded. Because there was no knowledge of evil, the first couple experienced a relationship that no other couple since has enjoyed. They did not know at the beginning of Satan's power to destroy or impair everything that is beautiful. We, too, have our moments of paradise, but the knowledge of evil lurks and its influence permeates society. How we all wish for the original relationship where there was no knowledge of evil!

The Fall

Now the serpent was more crafty than any beast of the field which the Lord God had made. And he said to the woman, "Indeed, has God said, 'You shall not eat from any tree of the garden'?" And the woman said to the serpent, "From the fruit of the trees of the garden we may eat; but from the fruit of the tree which is in the middle of the garden, God has said, 'You shall not eat from it or touch it, lest you die'." And the serpent said to the woman, "You surely shall not die! For God knows that in the day you eat from it your eyes will be opened, and you will be like God, knowing good and evil." When the woman saw that the tree was good for food, and that it was a delight to the eyes, and that the tree was desirable to make one wise, she took from its fruit and ate; and she gave also to her husband with her, and he ate (Genesis 3:1-6).

Most of us are familiar with the temptation and its consequences. Let's see if we might dig up some new thoughts, as we rake over the word. New truths ever await the "pearl-seeker."

Eve knew God's instruction to not eat of the forbidden tree and she was warned of the consequences if she did eat. But she ate. She was tempted and she ate. Satan fired his triple-barrel shotgun at her; his best shots. Shot one, the lust of the eye (it looks good), shot two, the lust of the flesh (it tastes good), and shot number three – (it will make you as smart as God) – the appeal to pride. Two thirds of the promise seemed to be true for it did look and taste good, but the last third had enough power in it to lose her soul. It did *not* give her the wisdom of God, but the wisdom of the world. Her actions separated her that day from God's presence. She was *wiser*, all right. She had the wisdom of the caught criminal who finds that crime does not pay.

Eve used her worldly wisdom to tempt her husband. Isn't this fruit pretty? It really tastes good, and look, I'm not dead and you won't be either. Adam was not deceived, he just ate.

It is amazing how many people think that Eve was "sentenced" by God to be *from that time on* the helper and that all women would enter a master-slave relationship because of Eve's surrender to Satan's trap. Her relationship, however, stayed the same with her husband. God did not say, "Now that you have sinned you will be Adam's slave." Eve was still to be cleaved to, loved, and protected. Adam understood this.

"To the woman He said, 'I will greatly multiply your pain in childbirth. In pain you shall bring forth children; yet your desire shall be for your husband, and he shall rule over you (Genesis 3:16). God's sentence for her was that her pain would be multiplied in child bearing. If she had not sinned her pain and ours would be much less. It would be like other animals as they bear their young. God complicated her labor pains and reminded her of whom she was, the

11

helper. Submission is not punishment. *Pain is punishment!*

Sin is always punished or God would not be just. "The day you eat from it you will die.", God had said. It took me years to understand this. They ate and were still alive, physically. However, they were dead that day, spiritually, cut off from God. God no longer walked with them in the cool of the evening. Man cut off the relationship, but God wasn't through with man. God wanted him back, and in His mercy He supplied the way to walk with Him again. Animal sacrifices would have to do until the perfect Lamb would be offered, the Lamb without spot or blemish, Jesus.

On that day (of disobedience to God) they did begin to die physically and in time man's days would number only one hundred and twenty years (Genesis 6:3).

God reminded Eve of her original role after she sinned ("and he-Adam-will rule over you"). If sin had never come into the world and that pair were still alive the rule would still be Adam's and his helper would still be Eve. Women displease God when they will not be their husband's helper in all that is good.

God did not place on her a punishment too hard to bear. Rather, He exemplified His awareness of the woman's physical makeup in His judgement. He dealt with her "according to knowledge". After all, He knows her strengths and weaknesses because He fashioned her with His own hands. "Your pain shall be increased in child-birth." This is enough punishment but we can survive it. We dread it and wish that it did not have to be so, but it is not more than we can bear.

God also reminds her that "her desire shall be for her husband." One version says, "Her desire shall be to please her husband." This is not punishment. This is a help to man and woman. Though you are to be submissive, you will want to be. (Oh, that we *all* wanted to be submissive where we are supposed to be, in the home, the school, government, and the church)! He placed in women the absence of competition and vying for supremacy. He wants her to assume the feminine role of the soft hen and to allow the roostership to her husband. He wants her to desire peace, so He places within her the desire (which we can stifle) to please her husband.

If God had placed on women the punishment He placed on men, few women would live long.

Adam's Punishment

Then to Adam He said, "Because you have listened to the voice of your wife, and have eaten from the tree about which I commanded you, saying, 'You shall not eat from it'; Cursed is the ground because of you; in toil you shall eat of it all the days of your life. Both thorns and thistles it shall grow for you; and you shall eat the plants of the field; by the sweat of your face you shall eat bread, till you return to the ground, because from it you were taken; for you are dust, and to dust you shall return" (Genesis 3:17-19).

It is interesting that God used ninety-eight words to sentence the leader, twenty-nine to sentence the helper, sixty nine to condemn the tempter. Why? Probably because God always expects more from the one in authority. He expects more from the parents than the children and more from the husband than the wife. We do too. We expect more from the president than the voters, the principal than the teachers, etc. And God expects *no* good from Satan!

Adam, what was your punishment? God complicated your labor pains, too. You were already working in the garden, and it was a pleasant work. Now it won't always be pleasant work for there will be thistles and sweat, and the duration is a life-time sentence. Your role hasn't changed, you are still the leader; it is just going to be harder.

Eve, your role hasn't changed. You will still be the helper and the mother, but it is going to be a lot more painful than God had planned for you.

Which of the two punishments would *you* choose for yourself? The pain of childbirth can be terrible, I know. But the pain doesn't last forever. And after it's over it's worth it, because of what they place in your arms. "Whenever a woman is in travail she has sorrow, because her hour has come; but when she gives birth to the child, she remembers the anguish no more, for joy that a child has been born into the world" (John 16:21).

Personally, I would take the sentence placed on Eve though I have a low level of pain tolerance. (Zero!) There is less constant pain in being a helper! The man's sentence is daily sweat, daily thistles until he dies and returns to the ground. Not only does the man have to toil

13

for himself, but for his family. *This is a hard sentence!* My heart goes out to him!

It seems to me that it behooves us, sisters, to make the home a place worth working for . . . a haven from the storms, a place of refuge. How every man must long for a place of comfort and love and appreciation for his thistled labor! In these days of multiplied divorces, broken homes, and shattered dreams, how blessed the man who has a helper like the one God had in mind when He gave Eve to Adam. We need to be one of those women, precious in His sight, and remember, though the word husband means the encircler, that men need to be encircled, too, with love and respect.

I doubt that Adam or Eve were giving much thought to her role of submission when she was brought to Adam, presented by God. I can't imagine Adam saying to his lovely bride, "Now the first thing we are going to have to do is to get our roles straight. I'm the head and you're the helper, and the first time you get out of place . . ."

However, some words *had* to be said after the fall and God said them all. "Your desire shall be for your husband and he shall rule over you." Her role had not changed, but she was reminded that the final say belonged to him. *It has to belong to somebody!* It has always been Adam's. God gives us two reasons for Eve to be the helper; we find them in 1 Timothy 2:13,14. "For it was Adam who was first created, and then Eve. And it was not Adam who was deceived, but the woman being quite deceived, fell into transgression."

Somebody has to have the final say; it makes sense that it should be the leader. May I take this opportunity to say to any man who might read this book, that this is the way most women want it, no matter how our liberated sisters may protest. *We love to be the held and not the head,* the protected and not the protector. We really don't want to make your living but your loving. We need the security of knowing that you love us as Christ loved the church and would die for us. "Husbands, love your wives just as Christ also loved the church and gave Himself up for her" (Ephesians 5:25).

You are our security blanket. You may not believe it, but many times when we seem to challenge your headship, we hope you will win. Women admire the strength and wisdom of a wise man. We not only admire it; we need it!

It's true that we might be able to manipulate the family buggy for awhile. (Pity the widow who has to drive and manage the kids at the same time.) However, we would rather that you handle those horses of "daily difficulties." Please drive, please.

14

After all, how many women want to be the leader, the sweaty thistle-puller, the decision-maker, the harried, tired business man and the place where the buck stops? Not me!

And what woman wants to be the sort who does not desire to please her husband, but wants to live with a mad boss? Not me. I surrender. That's a white flag in my hand. (The woman in the lead is miserable. God's way is the best way.)

God loved Eve. He still does. He loved her before she sinned and after. Aren't we glad? Because we are sinners, too, and we want to know that He loves us. He walked for a time with her and I know that she always missed those times after He left. He is going to let us walk again with Him, someday, forever.

Eve, you'll be so in demand in eternity. I probably won't get to talk to you for several centuries as man counts time. But that is one of the greats in heaven, there's no hurry! "When we've been there ten thousand years, bright shining as the sun, we've no less days to sing His praise than when we first begun."

To The Men In Our Lives

To our fathers, our brothers, and our husbands, too.
We have a request to make of you.

Would you learn to love us and let us be part,
Of the dearest dreams you hold in your heart?

We live in a world of temptations galore-
To cheapen our bodies, our thoughts and our mores.

The custom of many is to leave their domain.
To leave their small children, a living to gain.

But God asked you men the living to make
And mothers be home for everyone's sake.

To love us, defend us, with the dragons to wrestle,
To remember, dear ones, we're the weaker vessel.

Lea Fowler

15

Chapter 2

THE PRINCESS

God chose Sarah as an example to Christian women. He holds her up and says, in effect, be like Sarah. Well, Sarah, what were you like? What did you *do* to win God's approval?

> In the same way, you wives, be submissive to your own husbands so that even if any of them are disobedient to the word, they may be won without a word by the behavior of their wives, as they observe your chaste and respectful behavior. And let not your adornment be merely external—braiding the hair, and wearing gold jewelry, or putting on dresses; but let it be the hidden person of the heart, with the imperishable quality of a gentle and quiet spirit, which is precious in the sight of God. For in this way in former times the holy women also, who hoped in God, used to adorn themselves, being submissive to their own husbands. Thus Sarah obeyed Abraham, calling him lord, and you have become her children if you do what is right without being frightened by any fear (1 Peter 3:1-6).

So Sarah was chaste, respectful, adorned the inside of herself as well as the outer, had a gentle and quiet spirit, hoped in God, and was not full of fears. She was submissive to her husband and obeyed him; she called him lord.

At first she was called Sarai, which means princess, my princess. She was a half-sister of Abram and was ten years younger. They had the same father, which was permitted before the law of Moses was given. No doubt, she *was* a princess to her husband and a beautiful one at that!

17

God sent Abram from his homeland. He was the first missionary, so to speak. God sent him to a land that his heirs would some day possess. God sent him to the land of Canaan where he wandered as a pilgrim and a nomad for the rest of his life.

> By faith Abraham, when he was called, obeyed by going out to a place which he was to receive for an inheritance; and he went out, not knowing where he was going. By faith he lived as an alien in the land of promise, as in a foreign land, dwelling in tents with Issac and Jacob, fellow heirs of the same promise; for he was looking for the city which has foundations, whose architect and builder is God. (Hebrews 11:8-10)

Sarah went with him wherever he traveled. The princess lived in tents and did not complain. She had her own tent, for later on we hear of her son taking his wife to Sarah's tent. No doubt she had special decorations in her place and made it a place of beauty, for Abraham was a wealthy man.

The couple was inseparable. They had a lasting love for each other that saw them through many troubled years.

God told Abram when he left his home that he would "make of thee a great nation." That meant Abram was going to have children even yet, and he was seventy-five when God called him. Sarai was sixty-five. This great man of faith believed this was possible; so did his wife Sarai.

Sarai's Beauty

A famine came to the land of Canaan and Abram took his household to Egypt. He had many herds and flocks which had to have pasture and water. God did not tell him to go to Egypt. If he had asked God, he might *not* have gone.

Before arriving in Egypt, Abram made a strange request of his wife. "See now, I know that you are a beautiful woman; and it will come about when the Egyptians see you, that they will say, 'This is his wife'; and they will kill me, but they will let you live. Please say that you are my sister so that it may go well with me because of you, and that I may live on account of you" (Genesis 12:11,12).

Why would Abram take his lovely wife into a place where he knew that he might be killed and his wife taken into Pharoah's house? Was his herd that important? Would God have him put Sarai into such a predicament?

Sarai obeyed and God admired her for her obedience. This was a severe test and yet Sarai could not, or would not, endanger her husband's life even if it cost her a violation of herself.

I've heard it said by psychology students that the thing a woman is most afraid of is being used. It was spelled out to Sarai that she *was* being used. Abram said, "that it may go well with me because of you, and that I may live on account of you."

It did go well with him because of her. "Therefore he (Pharoah) treated Abram well for her sake; and gave him sheep and oxen and donkeys and male and female servants and female donkeys and camels" (Genesis 12:16). This was his "dowry" to possess Sarai.

Was God pleased with Abram's actions? We don't know. As far as we know, Abram is not scolded by the Lord. However, God steps in and protects Sarai. He brought such great plagues on Pharoah and his house that Abram is called in and questioned. "What is this you have done to me? Why did you not tell me that she was your wife? Why did you say, 'She is my sister'" (Genesis 12:18,19). The important part to remember is not whether Abram acted wisely, but rather how God took care of His Sarai. (At such a time as this today, He would still deliver His Sarah's!)

How frightened she must have been as she was brought into Pharoah's house and harem! Her heart must have pounded; no doubt she was praying to God desperately for deliverance. Would she ever see her husband again? How could he get her out of Egypt? They were friendless, unknown in that foreign country. Abram's wealth could excite the greed of the Egyptians. It seemed such a foolish venture.

Because of God's intervention, the story came to a happy ending. Pharoah commanded his servants to let them go with all their possessions. The pain of the plague did not make the price of the woman worthwhile. Abram left Egypt with a happy wife.

This was not the only time that Sarai's beauty nearly caused a tragedy. By this time Sarai is called Sarah, and her husband's name has changed to Abraham. (Sarai means "my princess," Sarah means "princess of multitudes.") It would not be long before she conceived Isaac. She must have been around eighty-nine years of age. The couple, in their travels, had come to Gerar. Abimelech, the king of Gerar, sent for Sarah because Abraham had said again that Sarah was his sister. (These were wicked men of an evil time.) Her friend, God, was not going to have this sort of a situation and he spoke to the king in a dream. "Behold, you are a dead man, because of the woman whom you have taken for she is married" (Genesis 20:3).

Abimelech swore his innocence and that he had taken her in his integrity. This was true. God acknowledged Abimelech's innocence, telling him "I did not let you touch her" (Genesis 20:6).

God did not let Sarah be touched for He loved her. He protected her and never allowed anyone but Abraham to have her. Again she had obeyed her husband in a difficult situation and caused her husband to be spared. It should be comforting for us to know that God protected His faithful daughter as she obeyed her husband in a life and death situation.

Confrontation

This loving couple had their differences of opinions, as most loving couples do. Sarai communicated with Abram vehemently and we have two of these important differences recorded.

Sarai reasoned within herself that she was too old for childbearing. (She was.) Abram wanted a child more than anything. So Sarai decided she would sacrifice her own feelings to help God and Abram to start a nation. This nation would number as many as the sands on the seashore, which are inumerable. When she advised Abram to take Hagar for a concubine, how heavy her heart must have been. Have you ever thought about what she went through when Abram went in to Hagar? Can we imagine the torture of knowing our husband was with another woman, even at our own arrangement? Surely she cried all that night, and many nights! As many nights as he went to Hagar.

She must have searched her husband's face intently and often. Was there any love for Hagar? Was she being replaced in his heart? Was there less love for her? Did he go into her room as duty alone, as she had planned? How she must have hoped for a quick pregnancy so the whole fiasco would be over. What dreams we dream and plans we make in vain!

The baby is conceived and Hagar has a smirk on her face. Women know how to vex one another; Hagar despised Sarai and felt herself the victor!

Sarai communicates, "Look what a mess we are in! What are *you* going to do about Hagar? The Lord is watching to see what you are going to do to this impudent maid to avenge her actions toward me." She declares, "May the Lord judge between you and me" (Genesis 16:5).

Probably what Sarai was saying between the lines was, "*You* should have stopped this foolish plan of mine. *You* should have firmly said that you would have no part of it. *You* should have said that you could never go in to another woman because you loved me too much. *You* should have said, 'If it can't be your child, I don't want any child.' Now get us out of this situation!'"

Abram replied, "Behold, your maid is in your power; do to her what is good in your sight" (Genesis 16:6). (This whole affair must have been offensive to this good man. Left alone, he would never have thought of such an idea!)

Sarai now has her husband's permission to say some of the words she has been rehearsing for some time. The words came quickly and hotly. (I'd like to know just what she said, but that is curiosity, and God did not choose to satisfy it.)

"Do what is good in your sight," Abram said. He might have been trying to appeal to the innate goodness of Sarai and to her mercy. Or he may have said it with the attitude, "It doesn't matter to me how you handle it." We do know that by the time Sarai was through with Hagar, the maid ran away in fear. When she came back, she entered again as a slave, and certainly not as a wife or concubine.

God saw it all. He picked up the pieces of the three lives and put them back together again. The foolish plan reaped its foolish reward, and God still carried out His original plan for Isaac to be born to Sarai when the time was right.

One can't help but feel sorry for Abram in all this. He was a good man, and our imagination can feel his embarrassment as Sarai, sparks flying out of her eyes, demanded the punishment of Hagar. In what an unenviable spot he was, between these two women.

Sarah was a woman, all the way, and God loved her because of it and in spite of it. Abraham did too. Sarah suffered for her lack of wisdom just as we do today in similar circumstances. God is not deceived; the reaping still comes from foolish sowing. Sarah paid for eighteen years for her failing to ask God what to do. God would have led her, if only she had let Him. Hagar's son was not a part of God's plan, but he, Ishmael, was born anyway.

Second Confrontation

This time, God intervened in Sarah's difference of opinion with Abraham. This time *Sarah* was right.

Isaac is born and Ishmael is jealous. He has been the only child all this time. When the baby is weaned, it was a day of celebration (Usually babies were three before they were weaned.) Ishmael is seventeen and is mocking and tormenting Isaac. Sarah sees it; this is the final straw. She has had all she can take.

She said to Abraham, "Drive out this maid and her son, for the son of this maid shall not be an heir with my son Isaac (Genesis 21:10). Drive out this pair. They are not fit to be in this house! Don't politely remove them in a subtle way, but *drive them out*, Abraham!

Now Sarah sees how perfect God's plan was, and His timing. Now she sees how bungling and destructive her lack of wisdom has been. How much trouble she has brought on so many people!

Ishmael was more Hagar's son than Abraham's. He was a "wild ass of a man" as God had predicted. His bad influence was not to be a part of that good family any longer. But Abraham loved him and felt that Sarah was wrong to want them to be driven away. How could *any* good man do this to a son he loved? Abraham was greatly distressed.

It was one thing for him to tell Sarai to do what seemed good in her sight to an impudent maid, knowing that the end of the situation would probably still have the pregnant maid as part of the household under Abram's authority. But to put out a teen-age son and his mother into the wilderness with no place to go was more than Abraham could do. So God spoke up and said, "Whatever Sarah tells you, listen to her, for through Isaac your descendants shall be named" (Genesis 21:12). Listen to Sarah, for she's right. God lets us know that in a difference of opinion, sometimes the wife is right.

Abraham and Sarah did not have a master-slave relationship, but a husband-wife relationship. She felt free to express her opinion. We know that she was a submissive wife. If Abraham had not agreed with her she would have had to accept his final decision, even if he was wrong. God showed him he was wrong.

This teaches us today that God has a way of showing a sparring couple which is in the wrong. If we are to be like Sarah, our attitude will be right. We can call our husband lord, yet disagree with him. We must be submissive in his final decision, but we can expect God to intervene on our behalf if we are right and the matter is of importance to Him.

God says that he wants His women to not be "frightened with any fear." God does not approve of any man (especially a Christian man) terrorizing his wife and misusing his strength. He will not have

God's blessings when he does this, rather, "his own prayers will be hindered" (1 Peter 3:7).

God wants His man to be the lord of the house and His woman to be the princess. When a man wants to be the lord of the house but wants his wife to be a Hagar, this man will not be blessed or happy. He will fail at helping to create a happy marriage and will "reap the whirlwind" (Hosea 8:7) as he troubles his own house. (It is easier for a man to treat his wife royally when he is treated royally.) Just as you cannot hide your light under a bushel, so you cannot hide a happy, contented home life. Everyone knows.

Sarah, we *will* emulate you. You were both holy and happy. You made a royal home for your husband even in a tent. You gave your husband not only love, but respect and reverence, which all men need. You were beloved by your mate for as long as you lived. God personally intervened in your life in wonderful and unusual ways because you were special. We want to be special too, and God says we can be if we pattern our lives after your example.

The last we hear of Sarah was after her death. Abraham goes to a lot of trouble and expense to see that she is buried in honor, her body protected in death. He took care of her in life and in death. "And Sarah died...in the land of Canaan; and Abraham went in to mourn for Sarah and to weep for her." (Genesis 23:2). Sarah was the love of his life. Abraham saw to it that she lived and died like the princess she was.

God saw to it, too.

Chapter 3

THE EGYPTIAN CONCUBINE

The way that God cared for Hagar intrigues me. She was raised in Egypt, no doubt an idol worshipper. Pharoah had given Abram some servants; she was probably one of them. There is nothing in her revealed character that draws us to her. She does not seem likeable. Yet God was mindful of her. God was kind to her. She was misused and abused, and God knew it and intervened in her behalf.

Abram was seventy-five years old when God told him to get up and get out of his home country, never to return. God promised that He would make a great nation from Abram's children, that his descendents would be as uncountable as the stars. This took a lot of faith, to believe that he would have such a family. He was already old, but Abram was that kind of a faithful man. He was called the father of the faithful, a great man of faith. Eleven years later, a son *was* born to Abram, but it was not the son in God's plan.

Though God had revealed that Abram would have children, He had not named the mother of the children. Both Abram and Sarai assumed that she would be the mother, although she had not been named. No doubt she began to doubt that she was a part of God's great plan. They were both growing older and were far past the age of childbearing and still nothing changes. Abram is eighty five now and Sarai is seventy-five.

So Sarai no longer waits on the Lord. She helps him out. She devises a plan. Abram will take Hagar; better Hagar's baby than no baby. She will be the substitute mother.

Abram would probably not have consented to this scheme except that it would give him the thing he desired above all else, a child.

25

And Abram said, "O Lord God, what wilt Thou give me, since I am childless, and the heir of my house is Eliezer of Damascus?" (Genesis 15:2). If only the pair had asked God what He thought about it! He would have told them. How much grief would have been spared to so many people! (Sometimes we don't ask God because we are afraid that He will give us an answer we don't want to hear.)

Nobody asked Hagar what she thought about it. She well may have thought it to be a great honor to be chosen. We do know that as soon as she conceived she became arrogant. "And when she saw that she had conceived, her mistress was despised in her sight" (Genesis 16:4b). Look at me, you'll never be the woman I am. I'm having your husband's baby, or should I say "*my* husband's" baby?

Sarai knew that Hagar was not a wife but a concubine. Hagar was still a servant though she had forgotten it. She thought her pregnancy gave her power.

"Under three things the earth quakes, and under four it cannot bear up....Under an unloved woman when she gets a husband, and a maidservant when she supplants her mistress" (Proverbs 30:21,23).

Sarai realizes now what she has done, the enormity of her bad judgement. She has "sown the wind and is now reaping the whirlwind." She has troubled her house. She handles it the way most of us do when we are wrong. She says to her husband, "May the wrong that I am bearing be on your head."

Poor Abram. The whole thing had never been his idea. He had been talked into a situation by his wife whom he adored. (He probably was not seeing the secret glances of mischief on Hagar's face). Now he has a furious wife who says it's all his fault and waits to see how he can rectify it.

"Let it be on your head." This just happens to be a little phrase that is often used in our family when one persists in going against the advice of another. We all hate to hear it, and it causes secret re-examination of our unpopular positiion. (I'm sure Abram didn't like to hear it, either).

Sarai has further words to say. "May the Lord judge between you and me." She is ready now to call the Lord in on this, but it is too late to alter the consequences. Sarai is telling Abram that God is going to see how Abram handles this. The Lord expects you to handle the lack of respect I'm getting from Hagar. What are you going to do? But what could he do, he seems to say. You started this, now you end it. "Behold, your maid is in your power; do to her what is good in your sight" (Genesis 16:6). (Let it be on *your* head).

Sarai treated her harshly. The words are not recorded, but by the time she was through, Hagar was back to being a servant. Not only a servant, but one who is the subject of wrath. Hagar ran. Most of *us* would have run, too.

It would be hard to imagine a woman in a worse predicament than Hagar at this time. She was a long way from home and her people. The wilderness separated her from any security of the past. She was a slave. She was a pregnant slave. She would need special care and consideration. She knew that Abram was not going to fight her cause and that Sarai was an enemy. There was no one to turn to! She even had the burden of knowing that her own contempt of Sarai had triggered this situation. Yesterday she thought herself impregnable and today she *is* pregnable! So she started out to Shur afoot. Can we sympathize with her? God did. How many times God picks up the pieces that our lack of wisdom has shattered!

God sends an angel to Hagar. First, he addresses her as Hagar, Sarai's maid. He reminds her who she is. He didn't call her "Mrs. Abram." Then the angel asked her where she was going and where she had come from. She didn't know where she was going, but she knew *who* she was running from. "I am fleeing from the presence of my mistress Sarai" (Genesis 16:8).

The angel gave her God's answer for her security and her predicament. Go back and submit to Sarai's authority. That was the only answer. The angel did not suggest that she go back to Abram for his mercy and protection. That would have caused a greater conflict! Only in submission to Sarai would there be *any* peace.

God did not stop there. Rather, His mercy and loving kindness went on to give Hagar something to live for, some comfort. He told her that the child she was carrying would be a son. God named him. "And you shall call his name Ishmael, because the Lord has given heed to your affliction" (Genesis 16:11). Ishmael would be the father of a great nation, though he would be a "wild donkey of a man, and everyone's hand will be against him."

The Lord gave heed to her affliction. She touched God's heart.(If *we* are going to be precious in His sight, our hearts need to be touched by those who are in the wilderness of sin. We must seek out the misused and abused and unloved of this world).

So Hagar went back to Sarai. We hope that she went back as a docile servant, appreciating whatever was given her, but I doubt it. I see two black eyebrows knitted, and a rebellious heart controlling a bitter tongue. There is no evidence of any friendship between Sarai

27

and Hagar again. Hagar's one joy is that boy, and he was hers to the end.

Sarai has become Sarah and God lets her know that she will be the mother of the "holy seed", Isaac. Sarah laughs at the news. God asks Abraham why Sarah laughed. She denies her laughter because she was afraid, but God said, "No, but you did laugh."

God knew when Hagar cried and Sarah laughed. If we could only realize the total involvement of God in the lives of His children! And that is not all that is said about Sarah and laughter. When Isaac was born Sarah said, "God has made laughter for me; everyone who hears will laugh with me" (Genesis 21:6). Thousands of years later we *do* laugh with her and rejoice at the birth of her son. The name Isaac means laughter.

Weaning day comes for Isaac. This was a big day for the people. Isaac was probably three years old. It was hard for Ishmael, no doubt, to see all the attention that Isaac was getting. So he teased him and mocked him, and probably had the child crying. Hagar probably did not restrain him. She might even have secretly delighted in Ishmael's actions. Ishmael is seventeen years old, far too old to be tormenting such a little one. This was the last straw for Sarah. Sarah was through with Hagar and Ishmael. She demanded that Abraham put them out.

Abraham refused, for he loved both his sons. So God intervened and told Abraham to listen to Sarah. It was time for Hagar and her son to go. This was a situation that had been tolerated long enough. Ishmael was old enough now to make a life for himself and his mother. Abraham obeys God with a broken heart. How he demonstrates his faith here! God tells him that He will make a nation from Ishmael. God is saying to Abraham that He will be mindful of Ishmael's future.

So Abraham rose early and fixed food and water for them and sent both Hagar and Ishmael away. How difficult it must have been! He did not know where they were going and neither did they.

Hagar and Ishmael wandered about in the wilderness of Beersheba. In time the water was gone, and she put the boy under some bushes for shade. She sat down where she could watch him and cried, "Do not let me see the boy die!" When she left years earlier, it is not mentioned if she cried, but now she cried for the love of her son, the only thing that she had ever had that was hers. She cried and he cried. They both were helpless and knew they would die in the wilderness without water. "And God heard the lad crying; and the angel of God called to Hagar from heaven, and said to her, 'What is the matter with you, Hagar? Do not fear, for God has heard the voice of the lad where he is. Arise, lift up the lad, and hold him by the hand; for I will make a great nation of him' " (Genesis 21:17,18). God opened Hagar's eyes and she saw a well of water. She refilled the empty flask.

Twice God intervened in the life of Hagar. Each time it was when she needed Him the most. There is no record or hint that Ishmael and his mother were faithful servants of God after their departure. However, God's mercy to an Egyptian servant and her wild son is to be meditated upon and glory given to our Heavenly Father who knows, sees, and cares about what is going on in this world of His. Yes, His eye is on the sparrow. It comforts us to see His involvement and mercy to those who did not live under His covenant.

It is encouraging to see the special care given to the faithful children of God, Abraham, Sarah, and Isaac, those who abided under His covenant. Maybe God intervened in Hagar's life not only because He is merciful to the Hagars, but also to help straighten out the foolishness of the Sarahs. How often we rely on His wisdom and intervention. How often we pray for Him to straighten out our well-meaning fiascos. And He *is* able!

Chapter 4

GOD LOVES BABIES

God is in the baby business! He loves babies and the kingdom is already full of them. Think of all the babies through the centuries that have died in their infancy! That's a lot of babies, and I am going to play with them through eternity.

Every baby is a gift from God. "Behold, children are a gift of the Lord; the fruit of the womb is a reward. Like arrows in the hand of a warrior, so are the children of one's youth. How blessed is the man whose quiver is full of them; they shall not be ashamed, when they speak with their enemies in the gate" (Psalm 127:3-5). How empty the home that is childless. I don't think this has to be. If we cannot raise a biological child of our own as we would choose, let's raise the child or children that God chooses for us. We can learn to love anyone who needs us. To raise the "unlovely" brings a much greater reward than to raise the one we so easily identify with, our own.

"He makes the barren woman abide in the house as a joyful mother of children. Praise the Lord!" (Psalm 113:9). God sets out some instructions for the godly women of the church to study and conform to. One of these specifications is to raise children. If God's woman will conscientiously adapt herself to this list of qualifications, she can be assured that no matter what happens to her or the economy, she will be taken care of by the church, by the Lord.

> "Honor widows who are widows indeed...Let a widow be put on the list only if she is not less than sixty years old, having been the wife of one man, having a reputation for good works and *if she has brought up children*, if she has shown hospitality to strangers, if she has washed the

31

saints' feet, if she has assisted those in distress, and if she has devoted herself to every good work."

(1 Timothy 5:3, 9-10)

"This is pure and undefiled religion in the sight of our God and Father, to visit orphans and widows in their distress, and to keep oneself unstained by the world" (James 1:27). There is not a better way to "visit" an orphan than to adopt him if he is adoptable. It is harder in these days to adopt an orphan than it was in the days the Word was written, but it is not impossible if we are not too particular. No wonder the Word says this is "pure and undefiled religion", for this is a very hard thing to do but oh, the benefits from having that kind of faith!

Let's look at a lady God blessed with an "asked-for" baby. Fervent prayer still produces some special children who grow into special, God-blessed adults.

Beautiful, favored Sarah, how she was loved by her husband! Yet, her greatest desire, to have a child, was unfulfilled. She said, "the Lord has prevented me from bearing children" (Genesis 16:2). And she was right. God wasn't ready for her to have a baby. She did not realize that God was setting up a childbearing situation for her that was unique. How many times our prayers are answered by, "Wait awhile; the time isn't right." In the fulness of time God brings about His will for us.

We're all familiar with Sarah's foolishness in trying to help God by giving her hand-maid to Abraham. We know the consequences and the problems that Hagar and her son, Ishmael, caused. In time they were driven out with God's endorsement and protection.

The angels came to visit Abraham and Sarah's home. Sarah eavesdropped. (I think most women would have in the same circumstances.) These were unusual visitors, and Sarah heard her name mentioned. The angels said to Abraham, "Where is Sarah your wife?" Upon hearing that she was in the tent, they said, "'I will surely return to you at this time next year; and behold, Sarah your wife shall have a son.'" (Genesis 18:10). Now Abraham and Sarah were not young; Sarah was well past childbearing age. Sarah laughed when she heard the message of the angels. She probably laughed in derision and unbelief. God talked to her husband about it. "Why did Sarah laugh, saying, 'Shall I indeed bear a child, when I am so old?'" (Genesis 18:14). "Is anything too difficult for the Lord?" (Genesis 18:13,14). Cornered, she denies she has laughed. She was afraid. "No, but you did laugh," God said.

32

The whole conversation makes me laugh. No doubt when she heard God's confirmation of the approaching birth, Sarah believed it, for it is said, "By faith even Sarah herself received ability to conceive, even beyond the proper time of life, since she considered Him faithful who had promised" (Hebrews 11:11). And this is not all the laughing we hear about in this beautiful story. After Isaac was born Sarah said, "God has made laughter for me; everyone who hears will laugh with me" (Genesis 21:6). And I imagine they surely did. Whenever anyone held that baby of those old parents, they must have laughed. Laughed in appreciation of God's blessings and power. Laughed at the pleasure and joy of the old parents.

Sarah not only had a baby at an old age, but she nursed the baby as well. Sarah said, "Who would have said to Abraham that Sarah would nurse children?" (Genesis 21:7).

There is so much laughing when a baby is in the house. How many hours we spend touching their cheeks and chin, coaxing them to laugh, and when they do laugh, we laugh, too.

Abraham laughed for joy when he heard that Sarah would bear Isaac. "Then Abraham fell on his face and laughed, and said in his heart, 'Will a child be born to a man one hundred years old? And will Sarah, who is ninety years old, bear a child?' " (Genesis 17:17). Sarah laughed at first in distrust, but in time with joy over Isaac. When Isaac was born, he was named Isaac by God. And what does Isaac mean? "He laughs."

Are you smiling as you read this? I hope so . . .

GOD LOVES BABIES

God loves babies and so should we,
Soft and sweet as a nursery.
Thousands of them are born every day,
Some are loved, some given away.

He has such hopes for their future life,
"Plans for their welfare and not for strife."
Wishes for growth - for possible dreams,
For parents to guide them down spiritual streams.

We hold in our hands the care of their soul.
We're so inexperienced and it takes its toll.
But if we keep on loving and praying for light,
God's wisdom will show us what's best in His sight.

For God loves babies and so should we,
They are soft and sweet as a nursery.

Lea Fowler

Chaper 5

God Loves Unborn Babies

If babies are gifts from God, do we have the right to refuse the gift? Man says yes indeed, and Satan says he thinks we should. What does God say about it?

God gives us an example of a foolish mother-to-be in the book of Job.

"The ostrich's wings flap joyously with the pinion and plumage of love. (Gavest thou goodly wings unto the peacocks? Or wings and feathers unto the ostrich? K.J.V.) For she abandons her eggs to the earth, and warms them in dust, or that a wild beast may trample them. She treats her young cruelly, as if they were not hers; though her labor be in vain, she is unconcerned; because God has made her forget wisdom, and has not given her a share of understanding. When she lifts herself on high, she laughs at the horse and his rider."

(Job 39:13-18)

The ostrich is wrapped up in her beauty, her plumage. She is impressed with her image. She loves love-making and her wings "flap joyously with the pinion and plumage of love." She gives no thought to the consequences of love-making, but thinks only of the joy of it.

She has no love for her babies. In fact, she doesn't care whether the eggs hatch or not. She lays them where they can be easily destroyed. It seems that she hopes for miscarriages. The eggs are only the unfortunate by-product of a love affair. "She abandons her eggs to the earth." She doesn't care how cruelly they are destroyed. If a foot smashes them or a wild beast tramples them, so what? She is heartless. She feels no relationship to the eggs; it is as if they were not hers.

It reminds me of Solomon's wisdom when two harlots came to him for a decision. Each had had a baby. One died in the night and they both claimed the live child. Solomon said to cut the baby in two, divide it. The real mother said, "No, let her have it. Don't kill the baby." The "unnatural" mother said, "Kill the baby." The unnatural mother still kills the babies.

I remember a kind lady many years ago who was having her fourth child. Her husband did not want the child. She went to the physician and asked about an abortion. The wise doctor, understanding the situation, seemed to go along with her request. However, he advised her for her own health's sake, to wait until after the birth of the child. She agreed to carry the child to term. When the child was born and she held it lovingly and tenderly in her arms the doctor came in. Seriously and soberly he asked her what method of extermination did she advise that he use? This good woman cried in shame, of course.

The ostrich would not care if her labor was in vain. How could this be? It is answered and explained, "God has made her forget wisdom and has not given her a share of understanding." As an example of what not to do, God made the ostrich like this. We know that God cannot be blamed for lack of wisdom if *women* act like this, for He made them in His own image and they should know better. God tells us here, spells it out, that it is the unwise woman who has no understanding, who is like the foolish ostrich.

He makes the ant to give us an example of industry and the grasshopper to show us the foolishness of frittering our time. He makes the ostrich to shame the selfish woman who loves to play, but hates the responsibilities of motherhood.

The ostrich sticks her head in the sand and hides. She hides her head in the sand and says there aren't babies in those eggs, and if there were, it won't hurt them when they die. She sticks her head in the sand of unreality and irresponsibility.

Our last glimpse of her shows that she is a "sport" but not a lady. She challenges a race, and she lifts herself high and outruns the horse and its rider. The eggs lie broken and the life in them dies.

She *was* beautiful, she was desirable, she was fun, but now she's gone. "Charm is deceitful and beauty is vain, but a woman who fears the Lord, she shall be praised. Give her the product of her hands, and let her works praise her in the gates" (Proverbs 31:30,31).

If there should be a potential "ostrich" reading this, could you find it in your heart to go ahead and have that God-loved baby and let some hungry Mama raise it?

You'll always be glad you did!

Chapter 6

THE UNLOVED WIFE

All of us want to be loved. We need love. Women flower with the springs of daily affection and appreciation. Some women receive more love than others. Some are more favored even from childhood because of beauty or personality. The baby girl is usually given much attention.

Rachel was the baby girl. Leah was the older sister. "Now Laban had two daughters; the name of the older was Leah, and the name of the younger was Rachel. And Leah's eyes were weak, but Rachel was beautiful of form and face" (Genesis 29:16,17). When you think of Leah, you do not have the picture of feminine loveliness that comes to mind when thinking of Rachel.

Jacob had left home, sent away by his old parents to see them no more. He knew they wanted him to marry a girl from his homeland as his father, Isaac, had done. His brother, Esau, had married out of the Lord and had grieved his parents. Jacob planned to be wiser. He came to the home of his relatives and saw Rachel. He falls in love with her at first sight. After he meets her father, Laban, he offers to work seven years for Rachel. Jacob has no wealth to offer, all he has is himself. Laban agreed and the time flew by. "So Jacob served seven years for Rachel and they seemed to him but a few days because of his love for her" (Genesis 29:20).

Think of those seven years. How he must have looked forward to supper time, when he could come back to the house and share a meal prepared by the sisters! How often Jacob and Rachel must have smiled at each other as they counted the days before they could wed. How pleasant to meet at the well and walk to the house together.

There was a lot of security in the way that the Jewish households arranged the marriage of their young. The pressure was taken off the young people in finding a suitable mate. There was a lot of comfort in their traditions, but not always equity.

You may wonder why Laban had not arranged a marriage for Leah. It could have been that her lack of beauty was a deterrent in finding a husband. It could have been that Laban was hard to please in selecting prospective sons-in-law. It could have been that he realized what an exceptional man Jacob was, and that he wanted him for both of his girls. Laban was a dishonest man, a selfish man who thought too much of his own wishes and not enough of the good of his daughters.

We don't know how much age difference there was between the sisters. Leah may have been enough older to have helped raise Rachel and to have had an almost motherly feeling toward this lovely little sister. She had probably delighted in the daily courtship that had been taking place. The sisters spent many a happy hour laughing and sharing talk about Jacob. Jacob had been a "mama's boy", the one his mother had favored. He understood women and felt comfortable with them. Rachel was his love and Leah was his friend, his sister. Leah was content during those seven years in watching from the side line. Her life was going to be in sharing *Rachel's* excitements, *Rachel's* marriage, *Rachel's* life, and *Rachel's* children. (Leah *must* have had an inferiority complex. It was inevitable.)

The seven years are up and Jacob asks for Rachel. "Give me my wife, for my time is completed, that I may go in to her" (Genesis 29:21). Laban acts like that's a great idea. He gathers the men together and they have a feast. Jacob is rejoicing at the feast and Rachel is putting on her bridal attire. Leah is helping her sister to make all of her breathless preparations. What excitement! Rachel was never more beautiful. The perfumes are unbottled, the food is prepared, the clean linens are supplied, but the bride is switched!

Laban brings in Leah! Think how that came about. Here is Rachel dressing for her wedding night; the sisters are busily doing the last minute things one has to do. Outside you can hear the men laughing and joking and teasing Jacob. Laban comes in and tells Rachel to take off her finery and Leah to dress for her own wedding. Imagination sees Rachel crying and storming as she tears off her soft garments and veils. Leah moves as a zombie as she puts on her best and goes with her father. If she *had* protested, it would have been in vain.

40

The room was dark, and Jacob thought he held Rachel. Leah was loved for the first and last time with whole-hearted love. But like her past had been, this, too, really belonged to Rachel. For a little while, she got to be the heroine and then she went back to a character part. "So it came about in the morning that, behold, it was Leah!" (Genesis 29:25).

How frightened she must have been! How embarrassed! Evidently, Jacob ran out of the room and found Laban. "What have you done to me!" Laban had his story ready, his defense planned. He told Jacob that it was the practice in this country for the older to marry first. One commentary I consulted said that was a lie. Laban could have betrothed Leah years before if he had chosen. Laban probably wanted seven more years of free service and his family kept together.

How treacherous he was! He wronged all three of the young people and paid in the end by losing them all as well as the grandchildren. He has his old age alone because of his selfishness and dishonesty. His life story didn't deserve to end right!

After a week with Leah, Rachel was given to Jacob, though he continued to work another seven years for her. "And indeed he loved Rachel more than Leah" (Genesis 29:30). Jacob knew it. Rachel knew it. *And Leah knew it most of all.*

"Now the Lord saw that Leah was unloved, and He opened her womb, but Rachel was barren" (Genesis 29:31). Do you mean that God in His heaven knows when a woman is unloved? He not only knew, but He did something about it.

Leah thought that perhaps Jacob would love her now that she had a son. Somehow she knew that God had given her this son, for she said, "Because the Lord has seen my affliction; surely now my husband will love me" (Genesis 29:32). She called the son Reuben, which means "see a son." See a son, but Jacob still saw only Rachel.

How many times we think our answer will be a simple one and that one happening will bring about complete happiness for us. How seldom it does.

We can visualize Leah freshening herself, swaddling the baby, and awaiting with joyful expectation Jacob's arrival to see his first son. Surely he will love me now for giving him a son! (Many marriages *have* been enriched by the birth of a son, but Leah's wasn't.)

So she begins to reason that if she has *enough* sons, her husband will love her. This is immature thinking, but we are going to see Leah grow up in time. "Because the Lord has heard that I am unloved, He has therefore given me this son also" (Genesis 29:33). She named him Simeon.

When she has her third son, Levi, which means "joined", she no longer asks for Jacob's love, but for his attachment to her. She wants him to recognize that they are attached, whether there is love or not. There is a marriage, and she will settle for that. Good for you, Leah.

We learn in time that things are seldom as good as we hope for in this life. There are always a certain amount of checks and balances. Heaven must wait. "Man who is born of woman is short-lived and full of turmoil" (Job 14:1). "It is a grevious task which God has given to the sons of men to be afflicted with" (Ecclesiastes 1:13).

Another son is born to Leah, and she says, "This time *I* will praise the Lord." The other three times she was bearing a son so that she would be more loved by her husband. She was having sons for him. This time she was having a son for herself and for God. Judah means "I will praise the Lord." Surely that was a prophecy of good things to come, for our Lord Jesus came from the tribe of Judah, and *we* praise the Lord for Judah, Leah's son.

Leah is becoming a realist. She is getting it all together. She probably thrust the first two little boys at their father constantly. She thought that if Jacob learned to delight in his sons that some of the glow would reflect back on her. This time she would not act as before. She would delight in this son for himself. And then she stopped bearing for awhile.

Now that Leah is beginning to solve her problems, let's check in on Rachel. The sons of Leah may not have gotten Jacob's attention, but they got Rachel's! She became jealous of her sister. This was a new emotion, to ever be jealous of *Leah*. Rachel always had it all. She now lacked one thing—a child—and characteristically, she *demanded* what she lacked. "Give me children or else I will die."

Jacob was angry with Rachel for her belligerent request. His anger burned against her. "Am I in the place of God, who has withheld from you the fruit of the womb?" (Genesis 30:2).

(Poor little Rachel. God did eventually let her have two sons, and who could ask for a finer son than Joseph? Oh, the jealousy that resulted from all the children and their rivalries! What mischief Laban fostered! What misery he brought on his own household.)

The last scene with Rachel is so sad. How hard it must have been to travel so far from home in such discomfort, and then to die bearing Jacob's last son, Benjamin. As she was dying she said to call him Ben-oni, which means "son of my sorrow." But Jacob changed it to

Benjamin, which means "the son of the right hand." Little Rachel was buried near Bethlehem.

Leah had two more sons and the only daughter. When the sixth son was born she said "God has endowed me with a good gift; now my husband will dwell with me, because I have borne him six sons" (Genesis 30:20). She is no longer asking Jacob to love her or to be attached to her. She just wants him to stay with her and not put her away. She seems to have found herself and be contented with things the way they were.

When you look at the end of her story, does it not seem to you that Leah's life became more meaningful and fruitful and satisfying? She learned to live without her husband's love. She learned to live without Rachel's love. No doubt her children and grandchildren gave her a lot to live for. She had the respect of the community, too, as the wife of a good man. God *always* loved her and looked out for her. As she asked for less, she really received more in peace of mind and maturity. She learned to accept what she could not change.

As I heard a wise woman say, "It is not what happens to you that matters, but the way you let it affect you." Leah could have ruined her life with jealousy and contention, but her last recorded words showed peace of mind. "God has endowed me with a good gift; now my husband will dwell with me."

God gives us all good gifts. "Delight yourself in the Lord; and He will give you the desires of your heart" (Psalms 37:4). He does not want us to let our minds dwell on the gifts we did not get, but rather to remember the end of the Lord. "You have heard of the endurance of Job and have seen the outcome of the Lord's dealings, that the Lord is full of compassion and is merciful" (James 5:11). When we think of Leah we should not dwell on "Leah, the weak-eyed" or "Leah, the unloved" but "Leah, the fulfilled."

As you ponder about these sisters, would *you* rather be Leah or Rachel? When we are young and more romantic, we would probably choose to be Rachel. As we grow older, it is easier to identify with Leah. God was more involved with Leah than Rachel. She lived a longer life, had a larger family, and died in security and peace of mind. Leah, the unloved by Jacob, but the beloved of God.

My life is but a weaving, between my God and me.
I do not choose the colors, He worketh steadily,
Oftimes He weaveth sorrow, and I in foolish pride,
Forget He sees the upper, and I the underside.
Not till the loom is silent, and shuttles cease to fly,
Will God enroll the canvas and explain why
The dark threads are as needful in the skillful weaver's hand,
As the threads of gold and silver in the pattern He has planned.

Anon.

Chapter 7

SAVED FROM A JEALOUS RIVAL

(Samuel 1, 2)

Few women living in America today could really appreciate Hannah's suffering, as bigamy is now forbidden by law. Hannah had a loving husband, but no children, and a spiteful, vengeful, though prolific "co-wife." Her name was Peninnah.

Peninnah knew that Elkanah, the husband, loved Hannah the most. This naturally, caused jealousy and where there is jealousy, there is rivalry and every evil work. "For where jealousy and selfish ambition exist, there is disorder and every evil thing" (James 3:16).

Jealousy cannot be appeased or reasoned with or mollified. Jealousy is an unquenchable fire. It continues even after the death of the "jealousee". "For jealousy enrages a man, and he will not spare in the day of vengeance. He will not accept any ransom, nor will he be content though you give many gifts" (Proverbs 6:34,35).

In other words, there was nothing Hannah could have done for Peninnah, or given her, that would have melted her heart and made her love Hannah. She *wanted* the love of Elkanah and the hatred of Hannah.

There was one way to get under Hannah's skin and torment her. It never failed to evoke the response that Peninnah sought. "Her rival (Peninnah), however, would provoke her bitterly to irritate her, because the Lord had closed her womb" (1 Samuel 1:6).

Year after year, when Elkanah would go up to worship and sacrifice, he would take the family and give all of them gifts. He would give Hannah double portions. And year after year, Peninnah would make Hannah so miserable that all she could do was weep, and not even eat. Elkanah knew why she wept. He tried to cajole and console her. "Hannah, why do you weep and why do you not eat and why is your heart sad? Am I not better to you than ten sons?" (1 Samuel 1:8). Is not my love enough? It might have been, if it had not been for Peninnah's cruel torment.

The Lord *had* closed her womb, but He knows what He's about. God knew that it was going to take special suffering to produce a special son for a special cause. God had a need for Hannah's son.

Hannah is desperate. Her husband's words do not help. Her prayers do not seem to have helped. She is at the end of her strength and is ready to break. She has endured all she can stand.

(Does God care if we have a rival? Does He hear our prayers while we suffer from the injustices heaped on us because of jealousy? Does He intercede in such matters? He did for Hannah.)

She turns to her last resort, the final place of appeal. She goes to the place of worship; she throws everything she has into fervent prayer. Her actions were so out of control that Eli, the priest, begins to watch her. She probably rocked as she prayed. Her lips are moving, but there is no sound coming from them.

Hannah is making a vow to the Lord. "O Lord of hosts, if Thou wilt indeed look on the affliction of Thy maidservant and remember me, and not forget Thy maidservant, but wilt give Thy maidservant a son, then I will give him to the Lord all the days of his life, and a razor shall never come on his head" (1 Samuel 1:11).

Eli thinks she is drunk, and he scolds her for coming into the place of worship in such a condition. She *is* beside herself, not from sin but from hysteria, because of the evil tongue of her rival. Hannah tells Eli that she is not drunk but rather is pouring out her soul. She is oppressed in spirit. She has been provoked unmercifully. Eli believes her and tells her to go home in peace. He would ask God to grant her petition. He didn't even ask what her request had been.

God would hear her now and she would have a son. Her faith was sufficient to believe what Eli had said. She left. She ate. She smiled. She could say with Job, "The case is before Him, and you must wait for Him!" (Job 35:14). She had cast her burden to the Lord and she had confidence that He had caught it.

In due time the baby came and she called him Samuel. This name means "asked of the Lord." She probably did not tell Peninnah that she was with child. Whan Peninnah finally knew that Hannah was going to have a baby, she knew that she had lost her power to ever hurt Hannah again.

The Peninnah's of this world, and they are legion, are the most miserable of all people. They feed on the hurt of others. Their joy is in another's pain, but their power is limited and they never really win.

How Hannah must have delighted in Samuel! She probably held him too much. Surely, she never complained of lack of sleep and the extra work that babies cause. She knew that she would not have him long, and the days passed quickly.

It was time to go up to worship and sacrifice again, but Hannah told her husband that she would not go up until the child was weaned. When that time came, she planned to leave him there. He would "appear before the Lord and stay there forever" (1 Samuel 1:22). Elkanah was an unusual man, for he told her to do what was best for her. He did love her, and no doubt he knew that God had given her this special child for a special purpose. No wonder Hannah loved him!

Weaning day came; Samuel is no longer a baby, but a little three year old boy, probably. The sacrifice was prepared... a three year old bull, one ephah of flour, and a jug of wine. They all went to the temple, the three of them. How many emotions must flood her heart: pride, joy, thankfulness, sorrow, and yet contentment, as this good woman fulfills her vows.

When she sees Eli she says, "I am the woman who stood here beside you, praying to the Lord. For this boy I prayed, and the Lord has given me my petition... I have also dedicated him to the Lord" (1 Samuel 1:26-28).

Little did Eli know when he helped the distressed woman to get her request from God that he was getting a helper who would never leave him, and become a greater man than himself. Eli was growing older and had only wicked sons who were a constant heartbreak to him. Samuel was always a joy and a comfort.

The story doesn't end here. Hannah is not just left with a memory of a little boy that she nursed, gave to God, and visited yearly with a new coat for him. Each year as they would visit Eli and Samuel, Eli would say, "May the Lord give you children in place of the one dedicated to the Lord." The Lord gave them five more babies, three boys and two girls. How they must have enjoyed these children. How Peninnah must have shriveled up inside with each new birth. What an unhappy furrow she plowed!

Samuel was dedicated to the Lord. Oh, that we would dedicate our children to God, and plan and encourage them to total commitment to Him. How many of us would rejoice if our children should leave us to take the gospel to the whole world? Too few, I am afraid. "Stay with me," is our cry, too often. Don't take my grand-kids away.

God was good to Hannah. She was the mother of one of the finest men in all the Old Testament. That's not all. She begged for one and He gave her six. He loves to give good gifts to His children!

Hannah's persecution at the hand of her rival worked together for good. No doubt it made it easier to give Samuel to the Lord. Peninnah intended evil just as Joseph's brothers did when they sold him into slavery in Egypt. God made it work together for good in such a way that Hannah was favored above other women of her day.

We'll probably meet Hannah and Samuel some day, but Peninnah will not be with the blessed unless she repented and changed her ways. It is almost impossible for such jealousy to wane.

"And the seed whose fruit is righteousness is sown in peace by those who make peace" (James 3:18).

Chapter 8

THE FOOL'S WIFE

(1 Samuel 25)

When I hear the name Abigail, my imagination pictures a beautiful young woman astride a donkey, riding for her life. No, not her life, but the lives of others.

Abigail means "joy of her father". Thank heaven for little girls! Maybe Abigail tagged her father's steps as he went about his business. Maybe she was a tomboy, for she felt comfortable on a donkey.

Jewish children were betrothed by their parents, and many a good girl was the victim of an unwise match. A rich man could have his choice. Nabal was a very rich man. He owned at least three thousand sheep and one thousand goats. Nabal was "harsh and evil in his dealings' (1 Samuel 25:3). He probably was so rich that he felt no need to cultivate friends. His money was his armor that surrounded him. He was accustomed to everything going his way. Nabal's name meant "fool".

Abigail was intelligent and beautiful. She was the greatest of Nabal's possessions, whether he realized it or not.

David, though he had been annointed king, had to stay in hiding, for King Saul sought to kill him. David knew God would give him the kingdom when Saul's time ran out. He had a large group of men with him who roamed the mountains, waiting with David for this time. They loved him and would have died for him if necessary. (This army was probably a pretty sorry lot of men, refugees, poor men who were off-casts of the world). They were camping near Nabal's flocks. David had instructed them to protect Nabal's possessions and take nothing. "They were a wall to Nabal both by night and by day" (1 Samuel 25:16). (They must have been tempted often to have lamb barbecue, but obeyed their leader.)

It was shearing time for Nabal. This was a great event, rather like a Thanksgiving Day. Large quantities of food were on hand for the shearers, and it was the custom to share with your neighbors the goodness of God's blessing on this occasion. It was right for David to expect some reward for himself and his fellows for their constant kindness to Nabal. So David sent some of his young men to him for a portion of the bounty. He carefully rehearsed these young men in what to say and how to say it. Imagination can see the men practicing the words over and over before they left, clumsy soldiers trying to be genteel and articulate.

> So David sent ten young men, and David said to the young men, "Go up to Carmel, visit Nabal and greet him in my name; and thus you shall say, 'Have a long life, peace be to you, and peace be to your house, and peace be to all that you have. And now I have heard that you have shearers; now your shepherds have been with us and we have not insulted them, nor have they missed anything all the days they were in Carmel. Ask your young men and they will tell you. Therefore let my young men find favor in your eyes, for we have come on a festive day. Please give us whatever you find at hand to your servants and to your son David.' "
>
> (1 Samuel 25:5-8

Note how courteously they spoke, how reasonable their request, and how deserving they were of what they asked. They did not ask for what they thought they should have, but left that decision up to Nabal. "Whatever you have at hand." Four thousand animals were to be sheared! A lot of food would have to be prepared for the shearers. It was a beautiful speech, and would have worked with anyone other than Nabal. There were no "right words" one could have used with this foolish man to make him share *any* of his possessions. Nabal's true nature came quickly to the fore. We see why God said that he had a harsh and evil nature. His first rudeness was to completely ignore them, the servants of David, and let them stand unanswered. "Then they waited." (Have *you* ever stood and waited after a courteous request? How dangerous to insult young soldiers!)

Finally, Nabal spoke, and his speech was worse than his silence. "Who is David? And who is the son of Jesse?" (1 Samuel 25:10).

Nabal knew who David was. Everyone had heard of the one who "had killed his ten thousands."

Nabal's wrath grew and his insults increased. "There are many servants today who are each breaking away from his master. Shall *I* then take *my* bread and *my* water and *my* meat that *I* have slaughtered for *my* shearers, and give it to men whose origin *I* do not know?" (1 Samuel 25:10,11). (Note the personal pronouns.)

Nabal's name fitted him! Any wise man would have known that you do not insult an army at your back door. There was no way that Nabal and his household could have defeated a battalion of trained men led by the greatest of warriors.

Such selfishness as Nabal exhibited is never justified nor tolerated by God or man. God does not let His own be handled in such a way without retribution. It will always be a "fearful thing to fall into the hands of the Lord."

> "In righteousness you will be established; you will be far from oppression, for you will not fear; and from terror, for it will not come near you. If anyone fiercely assails you it will not be from Me. Whoever assails you will fall because of you. Behold, I Myself have created the smith who blows the fire of coals, and brings out a weapon for its work; and I have created the destroyer to ruin. No weapon that is formed against you shall prosper; and every tongue that accuses you in judgement you will condemn. This is the heritage of the servants of the Lord, and their vindication is from Me, declares the Lord."
> (Isaiah 54:14-17)

The young soldiers turned away and left without a word. This showed wisdom, strength, and good training. They reported to David, who said, "Put on your sword." Four hundred men armed themselves. There was no sleeping that night, but rather an instant buckling of armor. There would be no peace until this matter was settled.

David's human nature had taken over. It is easy to understand and to sympathize with him although we hope for better things from David, the man after God's own heart. David's plan was for every male to be dead by morning who was a part of Nabal's community. (Foolish men can trigger even good men to be foolish sometimes.)

51

Nabal seemed unaware of what harm he had done. A servant, however, fearing that death was imminent, ran to the only one who might be able to help, Abigail. He told her how good David and his army had been to Nabal. "They were a wall to us both by night and by day, all the time we were with them tending the sheep" (2 Samuel 25:16). He asked her to consider what she could do, perchance vengeance is plotted against Nabal and all his household. He pointed out to Abigail that Nabal is such a worthless man that no one can speak with him. This was strong talk from a servant, but not a time for niceties.

Abigail, what *are* you going to do? Your intelligence has to pay off now for it is up to *you* to save your household. Abigail started running. David was hurrying and Abigail was hurrying. One was hurrying to kill and the other was hurrying to save that same group from being killed.

She gathered food, a lot of food; two hundred loaves of bread, two jugs of wine, five sheep already prepared and five measures of grain already roasted, a hundred clusters of raisins, and two hundred cakes of figs. What a feast! What a variety of food! The food was loaded on donkeys.

Young men were sent ahead to take the food to David. Abigail told them she would be coming behind them, but she did not tell Nabal that she was leaving. "And it came about as she was riding on her donkey and was coming down by the hidden part of the mountain, that behold, David and his men were coming down toward her; so she met them" (1 Samuel 25:20).

Here we see Abigail, the joy of her father, riding as fast as she could go, astride a donkey! At this moment she is not a rich man's lady, but a deliverer riding with hair streaming and heart pounding to try to stop a vindictive army. David and Abigail were riding as fast as they could go and they met head-on.

Again, Abigail hurries. She dismounted from her donkey and fell on her face before David. The first thing she said was, "It is all my fault. Blame *me*." What words, what *right* words to disarm David. She then revealed to David what sort of a man Nabal really was. "Please do not let my lord pay attention to this worthless man, Nabal, for as his name is, so is he. Nabal is his name and folly is with him; but I your maidservant did not see the young men of my lord whom you sent" (1 Samuel 25:25).

Note that Abigail called her husband foolish, but not wicked. She explains that he does stupid things and she is hoping that David will not want to kill a man who is just foolish. She also stresses that if she had been there, she would have been able to counteract Nabal's unwise decision and this wild scene would have never been played.

What wisdom she showed! Blame it all on me, if I had been there I would have been a good hostess and given you what you deserved for your goodness to us. My husband gets himself into predicaments like this because he's not a man of understanding. He doesn't know better, nor does he realize what wrath he kindles.

Her next logic is to remind David of what kind of a man he is. She says that God has kept him from taking vengeance into his own hands. God has kept him from erasing a small community because of the bad judgement of one man. God has kept an army from destroying a family. She lets him know that she desires his real enemies to be chastened, but of course it is inferred that Nabal isn't a real personal enemy of David, just a worthless man.

She offers the generous gift of food to David and his men. She asks again to be forgiven for her one sin of not being there to straighten things out. She asks for the Lord's continued blessing on David because he was fighting God's battles. May He keep the life of David "bound in the bundle of the living" and may He "sling out the enemies of David as from the hollow of a sling."

This was a very clever play on words, for everyone knew how David had used his sling to numb Goliath before he killed him by cutting off his head with Goliath's own sword. David knew all about slingshots! Then her final argument was, "When you become a ruler, you don't want a troubled heart because you shed blood without cause and avenged yourself. You want a clear conscience, don't you?" Her last words were, "When the Lord shall deal well with my lord, then remember your maidservant" (1 Samuel 25:31). When this is all over and you are blessed by your lack of vengeance and your good conscience rejoices, remember me, David.

David was an easy man to talk to. He was easy to reason with. He did not seem to have a pride problem, a too sensitive ego. We remember the time Nathan the prophet fearlessly condemned David for a sin and David meekly replied, "I have sinned." David could not only humble himself to a prophet, but could stifle his own feelings of revenge even in front of an army because of the reasonings of a woman. An army breathing slaughter in righteous indignation was calmed by their commander due to an intelligent woman. (David, indeed, was a man after God's own heart, while poor Nabal was a man after no one's heart.)

David not only changed his plan of vengeance, but gave three blessings to Abigail before he left her. First, he blessed God for sending her to him. Next, he blessed Abigail for her wisdom and advice. Finally, he blessed her for keeping him from person retribution.

He received the gifts Abigail brought. (Hopefully, these gifts help to gratify the soldiers who were denied a good fight.) And his last words to her were, "Go home in peace, see, I listened to you and granted your request."

Abigail starts home. The adrenalin has died down and the enormity of the situation lies heavy on her. What if David had not listened to her? What if she had had to ride back into her home and see the dead and the dying? There is no need to hurry now. She needs thinking time. How is she going to tell Nabal about what has happened? What will be his reaction, foolish Nabal, when he finds how much of his goods she has used as a gift to David? Is there any way to make him understand her wisdom in handling this life and death matter? Does she have to fear now for her marriage? Will he put her away, as he has the power to do? How she must have dreaded going home!

Other thoughts must come to mind. How will Nabal's pride handle the mortification of knowing his wife saved the men, even himself? How can he bear the looks of his servants as they despise him and respect her? His peers will laugh at him. Pride goes before a fall and foolish, selfish Nabal had never experienced such an humiliation as this!

Abigail arrives at the house and Nabal is having a feast and was merry and very drunk. Imagine, he was feasting while David was riding as fast as he could to kill him! He wasn't worried. He probably thought he had handled those men pretty well. He didn't know that his household was frightened for their lives, and rightly so. He just had himself a party. He who would share nothing with David was glutting himself with dainties that David would never have expected. Abigail went to bed.

Early the next morning, after he had sobered up, she went to him and told it all. Her words are not recorded. I'm sure they were wise. We don't know what Nabal's reaction was. We don't know if he realized the great error of turning away David's men. We don't know if he was angry with Abigail. We *do know* that God was there in that interview and that he protected Abigail! I used to think that Abigail must have been terribly afraid to come home and tell Nabal what she had done, because she knew better than others how cruel he was. I thought maybe it was going to be harder to face him than David and his whole army. I kind of doubt that now. She knew that she had done what she *had* to do. She knew God would bless her efforts.

"But it came about in the morning, when the wine had gone out of Nabal, that his wife told him these things, and his heart died within him so that he became as a stone" (1 Samuel 25:37).

The merry babbler is silenced. He sits as a stone. He sits ten days as a stone. What could one say to comfort him; could he hear if they tried? Poor, foolish Nabal. There must have been an oppressive silence in that house for ten days. Everyone must have been waiting to see the outcome. No longer was Nabal feared. All must have recognized *God's intervention.* And then, after ten days, God struck Nabal and he died.

God struck him. Does God strike every Nabal and free every Abigail? Probably not. However, surely, He gives the necessary strength to the Christian woman who has to bear such an unequal yoke. Nabal's sin was *so* great, David *so* beloved, and Abigail *so* wise that God did intercede. It brings to mind what Solomon said in Proverbs 29:1, "A man who hardens his neck after much reproof will suddenly be broken beyond remedy." Beyond fixing.

David heard of Nabal's death. One of his statements was, "The Lord has also returned the evildoing of Nabal on his own head" (1 Samuel 25:39). Then he sent a proposal of marriage to Abigail. The servants of David said to her, "David has sent us to you, to take you as his wife" (1 Samuel 25:40).

We see her running again. She quickly rose, rode again on a donkey. Five of her maids accompanied her. She followed the servants to David and became his wife.

There was no meaningless or hypocritical mourning for Nabal. She loved David and she knew it. We hope and trust that he always appreciated Abigail and loved her.

God blessed Abigail in many ways. Though she suffered a bad marriage to the wrong man, she pleased God by being a good and faithful wife to him. She was a worthy woman who worked diligently for the good of her husband and her household. God not only delivered her from an army of vengeful men bent on bloodshed, but he delivered her from a churlish and evil husband. Her story had a happy ending!

Abigail, Abigail, such a beautiful, brave woman riding on a donkey with hair streaming and heart pounding, I am anxious to meet you someday!

How different was this second donkey ride from the other! No longer was she riding in fear and trepidation. Now she is riding as a bride to her wedding with hope and excitement. How her thoughts must call the picture of David to mind.

Her last words to him had been, "Remember me" and he did, but more importantly *God* did. God made her a widow and then a bride, a bride of a king.

Chapter 9

THE INDISCREET BATHER

(2 Samuel 11, 12)

In the spring the kings go out to battle, but David, the great warrior, stayed home. His armies beseiged Rabbah, a city of the Ammonites, and the seige continued while David, the leader, rested.

One evening David rose from his bed and walked about on the roof of his house. He was probably bored for no reason. He had a family that loved him, many wives, and many children. He walked about the roof and he saw a beautiful woman, bathing.

Bathsheba was a woman of good reputation, married to an important soldier, Uriah. It was a hot night and to bathe outside cools one quickly. She was careless as she took her sponge bath, indiscreet. A good definition for discretion is to "do and say the right thing." There is no evidence that she knew that David had seen her, for it was evening.

For some strange reason, it seems easier for a woman to disrobe than a man. God calls women to modesty over and over but He does not have to stress this virtue to good men.

> "Likewise, I want women to adorn themselves with proper clothing, modestly and discreetly..." 1 Timothy 2:9
>
> "...your chaste and respectful behavior." 1 Peter 3:2
>
> "As a ring of gold in a swine's snout, so is a beautiful woman who lacks discretion." Proverbs 11:22

I remember several years ago outlaws took over a ship that had several Americans on it. The American women were advised to put on modest clothing for their own safety. (The men were adequately dressed).

We had some Korean engineers visit our home frequently years ago and they remarked how shocked they were by the brevity of the American women's clothing. They thought it immoral. When we visited the Holy Land recently, we saw a sign over one of the buildings; it restricted women from entering who were scantily attired.

Look at our own land. Watch the performers at the circus. The women are "barely" covered and the men are clothed from neck to foot. The same is true with ice skaters. At the beach it is usually the women who love the bikinis.

Bathsheba was bathing in an indiscreet manner. David saw her and wanted her. He sent and asked about her. Who was she? He found out whose daughter she was and whose wife she was. Although she belonged to one of his valiant men, he still wanted her.

We know what Jesus said in Matthew 5:27,28, "You have heard that it was said, 'You shall not commit adultery'; but I say to you, that everyone who looks on a woman to lust for her has committed adultery with her already in his heart."

A woman cannot be guiltless if she dresses (or undresses) in such a way that a man is tempted or has adulterous thoughts. If she is robed discreetly and conducts herself in a modest way and a man's thoughts are impure, the sin is his alone.

Women have always been in the "beauty business." It is not wrong to be conscious of one's appearance and to strive to be attractive. (However, to put too much stress on the outward appearance and too little on the inward is folly.)

"And let not your adornment be merely external—braiding the hair, and wearing gold jewelry, or putting on dresses; but let it be the hidden person of the heart, with the imperishable quality of a gentle and quiet spirit, which is precious in the sight of God" (1 Peter 3:3,4).

David sent for her. Did she want to go? She really had no choice but to go with the servant. She may have been frightened that Uriah was wounded or dead. It was not long before she realized that David had sent for her because he was interested in her alone. David, the beloved king, found her desirable! She was lonely; David was a handsome and pleasant man. *Now*, she *had* a choice, for David would not have forced himself on her. She probably succumbed.

If they could have known the price they would both pay for this night of love, they both would have run! There is such power in the magnet of sexual sin that you will probably not be able to escape it if you do *not* run. (Joseph, of old, ran leaving his coat in the hand of the seductress!) "Flee fornication" (1 Corinthians 6:18). Neither David nor Bathsheba fled.

Was this a one night rendezvous? There is no more mention of Bathsheba until she sends a terse message to David, "I am pregnant." A lot of men would feel that that is not their problem, rather, hers alone.

David tried to fix it. He called Uriah home from war. "Come home and be with your wife and think the baby is yours," was David's plan. (Sin is not that easily covered, especially when it is done by God's man, the "man after God's own heart.") David was not a young virgin seeking his first love. He was in his fifties, had many wives and concubines, and could have had many more if he had desired.

Uriah was pulled out of a violent war to come home and rest. Nobody else had a furlough. A thoroughly committed warrior, his heart was still in battle. David had him in for a talk. "How is the war going, how is Joab, how are the people doing?" Then, David got to the matter at hand, "Go down to your house, and wash your feet" (2 Samuel 11:8). Instead, Uriah slept that night at the door of the king's house with the servants.

A tired warrior lay on the floor and slept where the servants slept. Had he heard any rumors? Did the messenger that brought the furlough papers have a certain look in his eyes that spoke of volumes of intrigue? We'll never know. If he had just spent *that* night at the king's house, we would think he might have just been bone-tired from the war and the long trip home, and wanted to wait until the morrow to freshen up and see his beautiful wife.

Bathsheba may have been waiting for him, but then again she might not have known what David had planned. If she had known he was coming, it is interesting to imagine what she would have thought. "Will he look at my face and see the guilt? Has he heard anything? Which man do I love the most? Will my baby and I be stoned because of my sin? Will he think the baby his? Why, oh why, did I ever surrender to David?"

Someone has said, "Sin is fun while you chew, but after you swallow you have a stomach ache that won't go away."

The next day David arose with hope in his heart. "Is the whole fiasco over?" God did not let His chosen off that easily. This story was far from finished. It may not take long to sow, but reaping goes on indefinitely.

David discovered that Uriah didn't go home. Why not, Uriah? Uriah answers to the effect—"Why should I have it so good when all my companions are having it so bad?" He even says, "Why should I eat and drink and lie with my wife?" Then his last statement is, "By your life and the life of your soul, I will not do this thing" (2 Samuel 11:11). What thing? Go home and lie with his wife.

David gets Uriah drunk but even that does not work. Uriah never sees Bathsheba again. David sends him back to the battle-fields with a letter to Joab to place him in the front lines, assuring his death.

If Uriah knew of Bathsheba's preganancy and the affair, he might have loved her so much that he could not bear to see her again. He might have loved her *that much.* Uriah had loved her; David had lusted for her. Maybe he didn't care when he carried back his own death warrant. Maybe he was prepared when his buddies withdrew from him in the fierceness of the battle, and he was left to be killed by God's enemies. A brave man was killed because he had a beautiful wife whose indiscretion led to adultery. Oh, yes, the wages of sin is death indeed. And this was not the only death caused by that night of passion.

A short mourning period is set aside for the memory of Uriah. What a mockery of convention! What could people say to her at such a time as this? Friends that did not know, if there were any, could give sympathy. She knew she deserved no sympathy. (She may not have known that David had engineered this whole thing. She might have even felt relief that now she would not be stoned and would be married to David.)

David did marry her and they had a son, but all the time God was watching and writing in His book.

God sent the avenger, a prophet named Nathan. Nathan got right to the point. David, I know a wicked man who has done a terrible thing, and what do you think should be done to him? You are the king, you have the power of punishment. What should be done to this wicked man?

There were two men, Nathan said, one rich, one poor. The rich man had lots of flocks and herds but the poor man had just one little ewe lamb. This was an unusual lamb, for it was a "cade" lamb, a pet. It was raised up with the children. The man carried it around and fed it by hand and let it lay in his bosom.

Was there any likeness to Bathsheba in this story? Was she much younger than most wives? Was she raised up with his children? Was she betrothed to an older man by her parents? Was she a daughter-wife? Nathan says, "It would eat of his bread and drink of his cup and lie in his bosom, and was like a daughter to him" (2 Samuel 12:3). Nathan continues. The rich man was having company and he was too selfish to kill one of his many animals for supper, rather, he took this pet lamb and killed it.

Righteous David boiled, "He doesn't deserve to live! Such a man shall die and I'll see to it, but before he dies, he will give that poor man four lambs. He shall repay fourfold."

Nathan said, "YOU ARE THE MAN!" You are the rich man with your many wives. You took the daughter-wife of a man who adored her, babied her, carried her, fed her by hand, and gave her drink. You did worse than this man for you killed the owner. In a sense, you killed her, too. You took her good name, her reputation, and you have given her shame and heartbreak in exchange.

You, too, shall pay fourfold, David. The sword shall never depart from your house. You sinned secretly but will be paid back publicly. Your wives will be given to your companion and he will lay with them publicly. And worst of all, this little boy that was conceived in sin will be taken away from the two of you.

David's goodness came through. "I have sinned against the Lord" (2 Samuel 12:13). Notice he didn't spell out what had triggered the sin. He didn't blame Bathsheba. He didn't begin to excuse himself as King Saul had done when reproved of sin by Samuel. He was man enough to admit his sin and humble enough to realize that it was a sin against God.

Nathan told him that he would be forgiven, but "because by this deed you have given occasion to the enemies of the Lord to blaspheme, the child also that is born to you shall surely die" (2 Samuel 12:14). Then the Lord struck the child of David and Bathsheba, who became very ill.

Beautiful Bathsheba, how her eyes must have been horror-stricken! This was her first baby. Oh, how the stomach aches with the juices of sin turning and foaming in it! This sin of the guilty will fall upon the guiltless. The guilty parents will live and the guiltless child will die.

Bathsheba's future son, Solomon, will someday say, "The one who commits adultery with a woman is lacking sense; he who would destroy himself does it. Wounds and disgrace he will find, and his reproach will not be blotted out" (Proverbs 6:32,33).

The son dies. David says after his death, "Can I bring him back again? I shall go to him, but he will not return to me" (2 Samuel 12:23).

What a sad story! What a waste! What a payment for sin! Oh, that we may hide this in our heart and run, run, when we are tempted!

But how does the goodness of God to women come into this drama? Let us go on.

David then comforted his wife, Bathsheba. What did you say to her, David? Her eyes are puffed from crying. Her heart is broken. Her arms are empty. The beautiful figure is probably not so full now. Dark circles are under her eyes. The little ewe lamb is now a mother sheep with no little lamb. Did he say, "Bathsheba, forgive me—I should have done better? I let lust overpower my good judgment. We are going to start over, you and me. We are going to pick up the pieces and start anew. God will give us other children, hopefully, and we will spend the rest of our lives trying to make up to God for our sin and our foolishness?" We don't know what he said but he did comfort her.

God didn't tell David to put Bathsheba away. She stayed as his wife. (David would have put her away if God had commanded it.) He also blessed her with other children. She was the mother of the wisest man of the Old Testament, Solomon. God gave her a great, great son to take the place of the one who died. (God did not deal with another of David's wives so generously. Michal, daughter of Saul, put David down for his humility to God. God punished her by *not* allowing her children. "And Michal the daughter of Saul had no children to the day of her death" (2 Samuel 6:23).

And this is not all. Bathsheba and David had a son whom they named Nathan for the brave prophet. This boy is in the lineage of Christ (Luke 3:31).

David had many wives, but God chose Bathsheba to be in the blood line of His own precious Son. God knew the whole story of Bathsheba. He knew her heart, her repentance, and her sorrow. In His mercy and understanding He gave her a happy ending.

Bathsheba, we have doubts about Solomon's faithfulness to the end and know little about Nathan's life, but we do know that you had one son that you would see again for sure; that little boy who helped settle your debt. Too many of us have been too hard on you.

Chapter 10

WIDOWS

"Wash yourselves, make yourselves clean; remove the evil of your deeds from My sight. Cease to do evil, learn to do good; seek justice, reprove the ruthless; defend the orphan, plead for the widow" (Isaiah 1:16,17).

Widows touch the heart and compassion of God as do their children and orphans. David gives us the thoughts of God about them when he says, "A father of the fatherless and a judge for the widows, is God in His holy habitation. God makes a home for the lonely; He leads out the prisoners into prosperity, only the rebellious dwell in a parched land" (Psalm 68:5,6).

The Sidonian Widow

One of my favorite widow-stories is found in 1 Kings 17. In chapter sixteen we met Ahab, the king. "Thus Ahab did more to provoke the Lord God of Israel than all the kings of Israel who were before him" (1 Kings 16:33).

Ahab married the meanest woman in the world, Jezebel! She was a princess of Sidon. Sidon was the first nation to worship Ashtoreth, the female goddess who soon won the hearts of many Israelites, Solomon included. "For Solomon went after Ashtoreth the goddess of the Sidonians" (1 Kings 11:5). (His foreign wives caused this.)

Ahab and Jezebel were meant for each other. What evil the two of them perpetrated and enjoyed. How their evil influence lived on through their children!

We meet the prophet Elijah for the first time. We have the greatest sinners confronted by the greatest prophet of the Old

Testament. His family tree is not revealed. In fact, he is rather like Melchizedek, without father, mother, or descent. Some Jews have fancied that he was an angel sent to handle this infamous couple! (That is an intriguing idea especially, as Elijah did not die but was caught up to God by a fiery chariot.) However the scriptures teach he was of the settlers of Gilead, which would make him of either the tribe of Gad or Manasseh. He is called a Tishbite from Tishbe.

Elijah shows up uninvited with a threat to Ahab. "As the Lord, the God of Israel lives, before whom I stand, surely there shall be neither dew nor rain these years, except by my word" (1 Kings 17:1). For three years and a half it did *not* rain. Elijah was predicting a famine because of Ahab's wicked ways.

Ahab may have thought Elijah a false prophet or even a mad man. He seemed unafraid or affected by this serious threat to his country and people.

God tells Elijah to go to a brook. The ravens will feed you and you will have food and water. He chose the brook Cherith. Sure enough, the ravens fed him twice daily, bread and meat. (It is interesting to think of ravens, birds of prey, feeders of carrion, chosen to feed God's man proper food, kosher.) Ravens neglect their own but they did not neglect Elijah. Where did they get the bread and meat? Just another of God's miracles, no harder to supply than manna or quails.

The brook dried up and the Lord knew it, for He told Elijah to go to Zarephath in Sidon, for "I have commanded a widow there to provide for you" (1 Kings 17:9).

Here we find God "turning things upside down" again. He is sending His prophet to a *Gentile* widow. (Paul wasn't the first preacher to the Gentiles.)

God, in His providence, has her at the gate. She was poor, very poor, but industrious. She had no fuel but was picking up sticks in the city to prepare for her last meal. He asked her for a drink, for a little water in a jar. He knew that water was scarce and asked only for a little. As she started for the water, he asked for a piece of bread, too. She said, "As the Lord your God lives, I have no bread, only a handful of flour in the bowl and a little oil in the jar; and behold, I am gathering a few sticks that I may go in and prepare for me and my son, that we may eat it and die" (1 Kings 17:12).

Elijah said, don't be afraid, make your little bread cake, give it to me first, then you can make another for you and your son. For God told me, "The bowl of flour shall not be exhausted, nor shall the jar of oil be empty, until the day that the Lord sends rain on the face of the earth" (1 Kings 17:14).

This was certainly a test of faith. If Elijah had said, you and your son eat the first cake and then I will take one made out of what is left, that would have been far easier to do. What would she have to lose by eating the cake that she was already contemplating to fix? But God had said, "I have commanded her to provide for you." Somehow, she knew that she must do as Elijah requested and she did. She was a God-picked Gentile woman.

It wasn't hard for Elijah to believe that there would be continuous flour and oil, for he was a man of God and had been fed for some time in a much more unusual way than a woman making bread. He knew nothing was too difficult for God.

Sure enough, the flour and the oil did not run out. God did not instantly give her bins of flour and cruses of oil but made them walk by faith daily. Each day there was just enough for that day. Each day He gave them their daily bread just as He supplies ours.

Tragedy struck! The little boy died. All that mattered to her died. Her first reaction was to blame Elijah. "What do I have to do with you, O man of God? (1 Kings 17:18). Who asked you to come and seek me out? We would have both been long dead except for your arrival.

How quickly we blame God when a child dies! A death out of season. We are not surprised when a criminal is struck down suddenly. "Men of bloodshed and deceit will not live out half their days" (Psalm 55:23). But a child, an only child, how can we bear it? Her next thought was to blame herself. "You could have come to bring *my* iniquity to remembrance" (1 Kings 17:18).

Aren't both of these reactions normal when grief or death unexpectedly happens—it is God's fault or it happened because of my sins?

Had she been an idol worshipper? Probably. But there was something in her that made God protect her. Maybe she had been wise enough to see that idols are foolish to worship. "Hire a goldsmith, and he makes it into a god; they bow down, indeed they worship it. They lift it upon the shoulder and carry it; they set it in its place and it stands there. It does not move from its place. Though one may cry to it, it cannot answer; it cannot deliver him from his distress" (Isaiah 46:6,7).

Hopefully, as she and her son were fed miraculously each day, her allegiance had turned from an image to God Himself. Now, her guilt overwhelming her, she may feel that the boy's death is a reprisal for her idolatrous past.

Elijah is bewildered too. Give me your son. He took him to his own room and laid him on the bed. What to do? "O Lord my God, hast Thou also brought calamity to the widow with whom I am staying, by causing her son to die?" (1 Kings 17:20)

There had been no occasion so far in the scriptures of anyone being raised from the dead to live again. Yet, Elijah knows that with God, even this is possible. Three times he lays on the child as if he would warm the cooling body back to life. No doubt he loved this little boy. Then this man of faith prayed. "O Lord my God, I pray Thee, let this child's life return to him" (1 Kings 17:21). Let the soul return to the body from where you placed it. God, let the soul come back to the small body.

God answered Elijah's prayer. Was Elijah surprised? I hope not. He picked up that precious child and placed him in his mother's arms. "See, your son is alive."

Oh, the joy that must have been hers! How she must have wept and rocked him and kissed him, her little boy. We know just what she said, for it is recorded. "Now I know that you are a man of God, and that the word of the Lord in your mouth is truth" (1 Kings 17:24).

Elijah stayed there until the Lord was ready for rain to come. Did the widow and her son hold on to God after Elijah's departure? We don't know, but she had seen enough of God's power to sustain her faith for a lifetime. Her living son was a living testimonial to a living God.

Visit the Widows

"This is pure and undefiled religion in the sight of our God and Father, to visit orphans and widows in their distress, and to keep oneself unstained by the world" (James 1:27).

If you are a married woman you will probably be a widow before you die, statistics say. We need to be realists and to prepare for widowhood. We need to know how to drive a car, pay the bills, handle insurances, and restructure our lives. We need to have women friends, as we grow older, more widow friends.

God in His wisdom set the church up as a family and not as in the ark—two by twos. He says in this scripture that if we think we are good Christians, or if we want to be the best of Christians, we will visit widows and orphans in their distress. What does visit mean? It means, simply, what can I do to help? I care, I weep with you, I love you. You are not alone, for we are in the same family. We are related by blood, His blood. Our names are in the same book, the book of life.

God is aware of the distress. He seeks to comfort, and He does. Part of His way of comforting is to use a fellow Christian, a person, a real, warm, living person to show sympathy and helpfulness. When we become a Christian, we are washed, sanctified, and justified (1 Corinthians 6:11) and that word "sanctified" means set apart for His use. He wants to *use* us in visiting widows and orphans. If we are wise, and want to have "pure and undefiled religion," we will be *usable*.

Widow Cheaters

It is hard to believe that there are many people who will take advantage of a widow and try to grab her possessions because she is helpless.

"You shall not afflict any widow or orphan. If you afflict him at all, and if he does cry out to Me, I will surely hear his cry; and My anger will be kindled, and I will kill you with the sword; and your wives shall become widows and your children fatherless" (Exodus 22:22-24).

Do we have examples or other teaching more specific in the abuse of widows? Yes, we do.

"They drive away the donkeys of the orphans. [For themselves.] They take the widow's ox for a pledge. [Until she pays.] . . . Others snatch the orphan from the breast...They are exalted a little while, then they are gone; moreover, they are brought low and like everything gathered up; even like heads of grain they are cut off. [Those wicked ones who hurt the orphan and widow.]" (Job 24:3,9,24)

"Woe to you, scribes and Pharisees, hypocrites, because you devour widows' houses, even while for a pretense you make long prayers; therefore you shall receive greater condemnation" Matthew 23:14).

Note how in each of these verses the offense is stated and then the punishment that can be expected is spelled out to them.

Widow friends of mine have told me through the years how the world takes advantage ot them. Mechanics, plumbers, electricians, etc., etc., of the world know that they have no man to speak up for them and to question the bill that is presented. We read of the abuses that many older women have because of the neighborhood where they live. Many fear for their lives and are afraid to go buy groceries because of the young "punks" who will snatch their pocketbooks and beat them.

There will be an "Accounting Day" and there will be a payment in full. It is all written down. We can be sure of that!

It is bad enough when the world mistreats widows but when Christians, so called, abuse Christian widows, they cannot expect mercy, for there will be none. The widow cannot repay the cheater but God can and will. The cheater can expect his wife to be a widow someday. "And your wives shall become widows and your children fatherless."

Widow Insurance

God gives a list for Christian women to aspire to. Just as a list to the men who would aspire to the eldership, so one is given to the women who would be worthy of support from the church on a full-time basis, if necessary. It is a list of the "ideal", and the younger we are when we start trying for it, the better.

"Let a widow be put on the list (for full support and service) only if she is not less than sixty years old, having been the wife of one man, having a reputation for good works; and if she has brought up children, if she has shown hospitality to strangers, if she has washed the saints' feet, if she has assisted those in distress, and if she has devoted herself to every good work" (1 Timothy 5:9,10).

It has already been taught in the verses above that if she has children, they are to support her, but some widows outlive their children and are left alone. What a blessing it is to *know* that God so loves the older woman who has conscientiously worked for Him that He will see to it that she is cared for, one way or another!

The younger widow is told other instructions. "Therefore, I want younger widows to get married, bear children, keep house, and give the enemy no occasion for reproach" (1 Timothy 5:14). What is their insurance? God won't require them to do something He won't help them to do. He will help them to find a Christian mate, if they will wait for Him and continue to grow in Him. It takes two for a marriage, and even though sometimes a young widow may feel she is ready for another marriage, her God-picked mate may not be. We need to remember and be reassured that God is very time conscious!

God's Provisions for the Widow

"When you reap your harvest in your field and have forgotten a sheaf in the field, you shall not go back to get it; it shall be for the alien, the orphan, and for the widow, in order that the Lord your God may bless you in all the work of your hands" (Deuteronomy 24:19). It goes on to say the same thing about their olive trees and their grapes. Remember, I'm watching, God is saying.

"Cursed is he who distorts the justice due an alien, orphan, and widow" (Deuteronomy 27:19). Though we are now under a new and better law, we know that the same God will be seeing that His widow gets justice. The unjust will be handled by God. "A father of the fatherless and a judge for the widows" (Psalm 68:5). He will be the judge for the widows. No worry for fear that her case will be handled by a merciless and unfeeling administrator. He will call the shots.

"God setteth the solitary in families" (Psalm 68:6, KJV). God knows their loneliness. He will find someone who cares for them in a personal way. God will pick the family. Will it be yours? Would she like to be a part of your family, or would she rather be alone than to feel your lack of hospitality? Wouldn't it be lovely to know that God had assigned a certain widow to you because you are the one for her?

Remember when Christ sent out the twelve in the limited commission? He told them to find a house that was worthy and then stay there. Would we have had one of those houses? Christ told them that if a house was found unworthy to shake their feet. Do we have widows in the church today who are mentally shaking their feet at our front door? It is worthy of solemn thought.

In Conclusion

None of us know our future. We may feel secure because of several loving, grown children. We may feel we have no worry about a place to go if we become widows. "Cast your bread on the surface of the waters, for you will find it after many days. Divide your portion to seven, or even to eight, for you do not know what misfortune may occur on the earth" (Ecclesiastes 11:1,2). No, we do not know what misfortunes are ahead for us and how lonely we may be someday. I'm sure many widows would tell you today, "I'd do a lot of things differently if I could do them over."

There may be widows who read this and bitterly disagree with the words of God when He said, "I'll be your judge, I'll set you in a family, or I'll curse the one who mistreats you." They may say, "I have no such help. He hasn't done this for me!"

We need to realize that all of these promises are to those in the family of God. God loves *all* widows and feels compassion for them, but all spiritual blessings are "in Christ." (Ephesians 1:3) We need to place ourselves where the blessings are before the balm of Gilead can be poured over us and we will be healed.

"Come unto me all who are weary and heavy laden, and I will give you rest" (Matthew 11:28). That's for me, says the widow. I am weary, tired, and my burdens are too much. Where is this rest? He answers, "Take my yoke upon you, and learn from Me." (Matthew 11:29). It takes learning to be His, study, discipline, and obedience.

Did you notice all the words of comfort to the widow? This is just another example of God's love for womankind. He understands our needs, our limitations, our griefs, our strengths, and our weaknesses. He endeavours through His word to get holy people to be gentle and loving to those who need it most, the widows.

A WIDOW'S LAMENT

I am so lonely, I feel so lost,
I don't know where to turn.

My children grieve me, so high the cost
Of peace, I learn.

There are few answers, I'd like to go,
To close my eyes in peace.

But there is One, who is my stay,
Who holds my hand and points the way.

"This, too, shall pass," I hear Him say
And I believe the Son.

Lea Fowler

Chapter 11

THE DEPRESSED WOMAN

God made His people some promises when He gave them the land of milk and honey. He promised them blessings if they served Him and curses if they did not.

> And it shall come about, if you listen obediently to my commandments which I am commanding you today, to love the Lord your God and to serve Him with all your heart and all your soul, that He will give the rain for your land in its season, the early and late rain, that you may gather in your grain and your new wine and your oil. And He will give grass in your fields for your cattle, and you shall eat and be satisfied. Beware, lest your hearts be deceived and you turn away and serve other gods and worship them. Or the anger of the Lord will be kindled against you, and He will shut up the heavens so that there will be no rain and the ground will not yield up its fruit....
> Deuteronomy 11:13-17

A famine was in the land of Judah because of the sins of the people. Famines were often sent to drive God's people back to Him. During this particular dearth we meet a family, Elimelech and his wife Naomi and their two sons. Elimilech means "my God a King" and Naomi means "amiable and pleasant." Their two sons were nearly grown and they were evidently sick young men, for one was named Mahlon, meaning "sickness," and the other was Chilion, meaning, "consumption."

71

The family decided to move to Moab because there was food there. It proved to be a very bad decision, for it ended in tragedy. Often, people who are having a hard time financially search for quick relief and move hastily and unwisely. Elemilech's family did not ask God, as far as we know, about the wisdom of their action. (Their brethren remaining in their homeland did survive. Maybe they trusted in the teaching of God's word that said, "For His anger is but for a moment, His favor is for a lifetime" (Psalms 30:5).

I wonder who ramrodded this expedition? Could it be that Naomi had her part in the unwise decision? She had some sick young men in her home and no doubt thought they had to have better food. (Women seek security sometimes to their own detriment.) It never crossed her mind that Elimelech might die there, as well as the sons she was seeking to spare.

Elimilech did die. How awful to be a widow in a foreign land! What is she doing here? Why did they leave home? Who will mourn and weep and rock with her? Maybe now she tried to get the boys to go home, but they have wives and their own homes in Moab.

The sons die. It could have been that all three men picked up one of the communicable diseases of that land and died within a few weeks of each other. One of the promises that God had made to His people was that He would protect them from the diseases of other lands if they would be true to Him. "And the Lord will remove from you all sickness; and He will not put on you any of the harmful diseases of Egypt which you have known, but He will lay them on all who hate you" (Deuteronomy 7:15). The Jewish Chaldee says, speaking of the sons, "Their days were shortened because they transgressed the law in marrying strange wives" (Commentary on the Bible, Matthew Henry). It does seem that there was weak family teaching by word and action.

It brings to my mind the way Samson spoke to his parents when he chose to marry out of the Lord. "So he came back and told his father and mother, 'I saw a woman in Timnah, one of the daughters of the Philistines; now therefore, get her for me as a wife.' Then his father and his mother said to him, 'Is there no woman among the daughters of your relatives, or among all our people, that you go to take a wife from the uncircumcised Philistines?' But Samson said to his father, 'Get her for me, for she looks good to me'" (Judges 14:2,3). (It is a sad thing to see a lot of Christian grandmothers raising the children of the hastily married, hastily divorced, who married only because "She looks good to me.")

72

The famine is over. Naomi is going home. She knows now where she belongs. She is going home. She starts back and her two daughters-in-law walk with her. They loved her and she them. This speaks well of our amiable and pleasant Naomi. It also speaks well of the Moabite women. Naomi tries to get them to go back to their own homes. She gives them a blessing. "May the Lord deal kindly with you as you have dealt with the dead and with me" (Ruth 1:8). Naomi set us a good example in her dealings with her Moabite daughters-in-law. Though her sons had married out of the Lord, she did what she could to deal with them kindly and succeeded in winning their love through her love.

"May the Lord grant that you may find rest, each in the house of her husband" (Ruth 1:9). Marry again, girls, and marry a local boy and stay in your own land. This was good advice. Orpah listened, wept again, and returned to her home.

Ruth chose to suffer Naomi's lot. She said one of the most touching dialogues recorded in the Good Book and one that we are all familiar with. "Do not urge me to leave you or turn back from following you; for where you go, I will go, and where you lodge, I will lodge. Your people shall be my people, and your God, my God. Where you die, I will die, and there I will be buried. Thus may the Lord do to me, and worse, if anything but death parts you and me" (Ruth 1:16,17). Such words must have moved Naomi's heart and filled her with joy. She would not have to make that long trip alone. She would not have to live alone and try to provide for herself.

The two entered Bethlehem. The city stirred and the women asked, "Is this Naomi?" Heartbreak changes the countenance, the posture, the soul, and the hopes. No, this was *not* the Naomi who had left.

"Do not call me Naomi (pleasant); call me Mara (bitter), for the Almighty has dealt very bitterly with me. I went out full, but the Lord has brought me back empty. Why do you call me Naomi, since the Lord has witnessed against me and the Almighty has afflicted me?" (Ruth 1:20,21).

These words make me wonder if Naomi had not helped to persuade her husband to leave Bethlehem for Moab. "The Lord witnessed against me." He hears our plans, especially those that take us away from Him.

We cannot be sure that the Lord had done all of this. He may have. However, we need to be cautious about accusing God of every wrong that happens to us. Good and bad people die daily. Children

73

do many foolish things that take their lives. More accidents happen at home than any other place, but this does not mean these accidents are God-oriented. Though God is omnipotent, He does not choose to intervene in our every act. Though God *can* be punitive, we should not attribute to Him every misfortune that befalls us. He is a loving God and not a hard taskmaster. We need always to be aware of the fact that Satan has a lot to do with death. Remember who took Job's ten children. It was not God!

"I went out full—I'm now empty." She knows *now* that she went out full. At one time she thought she was empty and had to go to Moab to be filled.

"The Almighty has dealt very bitterly with me." Did you ask Him whether you should leave the promised land? Weren't you getting some negative messages as you packed up to leave your people and go to a land of idol worshippers?

Naomi thought all of her happiness was forever gone. *We can always be happy again, or at peace, no matter what tragedy befalls us.* Naomi finds this out. God shares her story with us.

Ruth went to work to support herself and her mother-in-law. She probably did the only thing that could be done by a young woman in need; she gleaned in the fields. God had ordained that the corners of the fields should be left for widows and orphans. It is said that you could tell the stingy man of that day by the way he treated the corners of his land.

Now Ruth "happened" to go to Boaz's field, a relative of Elimilech. Boaz "happened" to come to Bethlehem at that time and was in the field where Ruth gleaned. (These types of things are still "happening" to God's children.)

Boaz asked about Ruth and found that she had a good reputation. Boaz said to her, "All that you have done for your mother-in-law after the death of your husband has been fully reported to me, and how you left our father and your mother and the land of your birth, and came to a people that you did not previously know. May the Lord reward you work, and your wages be full from the Lord, the God of Israel, under whose wings you have come to seek refuge" (Ruth 2:11,12).

Boaz was Rahab's son. Rahab was a woman from a nation who worshipped idols. A former harlot, she was saved from death, with her family, for rescuing the spies sent by Joshua. She was adopted by a people who knew her not. She, too, was living with a people she did not "previously know." No doubt she talked to Boaz as he grew up about how lonely it was, and how she was raised separate from the people of God. Rahab did not start with a good reputation, but Ruth did.

Boaz instructed his servants to protect Ruth. He told her to stay in his fields. He told her to drink with his servants. At lunch time he had her come sit with him and he served her roasted grain. He gave her so much that she had leftovers. Then after she went back to work, he told his servants to leave her extra grain to reap, and not to rebuke her.

Ruth relayed to Naomi all the day's happenings. Naomi begins to think, as older women do, about matchmaking. (There is nothing wrong in Christians doing a little matchmaking. We need to make it easier for Christians to meet each other. Our homes and hearts should be opened to those of the marriageable age.) Whether she realizes it or not, Naomi is beginning to come back to life. There is nothing like romance to brighten the eyes and make life interesting again! Naomi loves Ruth and wants what is best for her.

Naomi says, "My daughter, shall I not seek security for you, that it may be well with you?" (Ruth 3:1). This was said after Ruth had continued to glean for some time and a regular routine had developed.

Why, oh why, don't more parents seek security for the well-being of their teenagers who are fast approaching marriage? Why don't we get up and out to see that our young have every advantage of Christian companionship that is available? Why isn't our home "open house" for at least our own (and others)?

One of the main reasons is that too many mothers are not at home themselves, and when they get home, they are too tired to entertain. The easy way is the lazy way and the lazy way often leads to ruin. Before you know it, they are gone. And if we have not done them right, they are *really* gone! God gives us our children while we are young and have the energy necessary to raise them. We *can* get up one more time. We *can* counsel at midnight. (Noah saved only his family, though there was room in that boat for many others. After a hundred or so years of preaching, wouldn't it have been awful to have lost his own kids?)

Back to Naomi. She gave some good, practical advice about how to attract the opposite sex. "Take a bath and put on your best clothes." It still works. Then she spelled out an unusual courting procedure. Naomi wanted to know if Boaz was really interested in Ruth, but she wanted to be sure it was done discreetly. Ruth must not get a bad reputation and this plan could have backfired easily.

Wait until he has eaten and drank. Wait until he is alone and it is dark. Wait until he has retired for the evening. Uncover his *feet* and lie by his *feet*. He will tell you what to do. The next move will be his. Naomi knew that Boaz was a good man, an older man, and that he already respected and appreciated Ruth.

Ruth did exactly as she was told. She trusted Naomi. Her heart must have been pounding as she laid at his feet. Her faith in Naomi was being tested severely.

Boaz awoke, startled, and asked who it was. She answered, "I am Ruth your maid. So spread your covering over your maid, for you are a close relative" (Ruth 2:9). She reminded him of his place. You are a *close* relative. She had not lain up by him to be taken. She was not offering herself to him out of wedlock. She was not tempting him to sin.

His answer was so perfect and showed what a worthy man he was. "May you be blessed of the Lord, my daughter. You have shown your last kindness to be better than the first by not going after young men, whether rich or poor. And now, my daughter, do not fear. I will do for you whatever you ask, for all my people know that you are a woman of excellence" (Ruth 3:10,11). God blessed Naomi's plan and drew two honorable people together. God matchmakes!

Boaz let her rest a little longer. I'm sure she had not had any sleep. She left very early, which was wise. He sent her home with food. (He had been feeding Ruth for a long time now.)

Don't you know that Ruth was not the only one who didn't get much sleep? There were three that did not rest well that night, Boaz, Ruth, and Naomi. When Ruth told her how it had gone that night, she answered, "The man will not rest until he has settled it today."

She was right. All that had to be done to allow the marriage was undertaken and accomplished. All legal transactions were finished.

Ruth and Boaz were married and they had a little boy named Obed, who in time had a son named Jesse. Jesse's son was named David, who was in the lineage of the child of Mary, Jesus.

The women gathered around Naomi when Obed was born and gave her a blessing. "Blessed is the Lord who has not left you without a redeemer today, and may his name become famous in Israel. May he also be to you a restorer of life and a sustainer of your old age; for your daughter-in-law, who loves you and is better to you than seven sons, has given birth to him" (Ruth 4:14,15).

Naomi held that little boy on her lap and became his nurse. As she rocked him and sang to him, the old hurts melted away. Bitterness was gone and was replaced with pleasantness once more. The neighbor women said, "A son has been born to Naomi."

If an old friend would have visited her then and called her "Mara", surely Naomi would have said, "Call me Naomi. I was empty, but now, again, I am full."

Naomi found that depression is not a part of God's plan for His children. *Whatever* depresses will only "come to pass."

THE MISSION OF MISERY

One truth I hold whatever comes to me;
This, too, will only last temporarily.
Storms fail, lightnings cease,
Troubles die, troubles ease.

Character is formed by our woes,
Not our highs—but our lows.
Wounds heal and tears do, too.
(What did trouble make of you?)
What are we worth—I know the cost,
Jesus dying on a cross,

When I suffer "I cease from sin".
Myself goes out and His self comes in.
So help me grow and help me heed,
Things oft go wrong just for my need.

Lea Fowler

Chapter 12

The CARPENTER'S WIFE

Sarah was like a princess all her life. Abraham was a wealthy man. Sarah had her own tent furnished with the best of that day. She had servants and whatever her heart desired in a material way.

Mary, too, was a woman of royal blood, for she was of the house of David, the king. Yet her heredity profited her nothing, for she had no servants and her offerings to God had to be the sacrifices of the poor.

Mary was engaged to a carpenter, Joseph, who also was of the house of David. Many think that Joseph was much older than Mary. God does not say. (The fact that Joseph is not mentioned after Jesus was twelve years old causes the assumption that he probably died before Jesus went into his personal ministry.)

Mary was a virgin. No doubt there were many Jewish girls of her age who were virgins, but it was time for the Messiah to come and the *right* virgin must be chosen. Prophecy had said that the Messiah would be born of a virgin. "Therefore the Lord Himself will give you a sign: Behold, a virgin will be with child and bear a son, and she will call His name Immanuel" (Isaiah 7:14).

Now in the sixth month the angel Gabriel was sent from God to a city in Galilee, called Nazareth, to a virgin engaged to a man whose name was Joseph, of the descendants of David; and the virgin's name was Mary. And coming in, he said to her, "Hail, favored one! The Lord is with you." But she was greatly troubled at this statement, and kept pondering what kind of salutation this might be. And the angel said to her, "Do not be afraid, Mary; for

79

you have found favor with God. And behold, you will conceive in your womb, and bear a son, and you shall name Him Jesus. He will be great, and will be called the Son of the Most High; and the Lord God will give Him the throne of His father David; and He will reign over the house of Jacob forever; and His kingdom will have no end.

(Luke 1:26-33)

Mary answered, in effect, "How can this be? I'm engaged, but not married, and I have never known a man sexually."

Gabriel answered, "The Holy Spirit will overshadow you, and the Holy Offspring will be called the Son of God."

Mary was a virgin when Gabriel talked to her and was still a virgin when her first son, Jesus, was born.

The angel told her that a sign would be given to her. Her relative, Elizabeth, who was called barren, was now in her sixth month of pregnancy. The fore-runner of Christ was to come six months before Jesus. Gabriel added, "For nothing will be impossible with God" (Luke 1:37).

Mary answered in this way, "I'm God's bondslave, let it be as you have said." God had chosen the right virgin!

Human nature would have been tempted to argue or delay her answer. Let me talk to my mother about this. What will Joseph say? He may not agree with you and I. I'll meet you later after I have discussed it with him. Mary did *not* react in this way.

Instead, this God-chosen girl started for Elizabeth's house. Only Elizabeth could understand Mary's miracle, because her own baby was to be born out of season, born to an old woman. She would understand and believe that even a virgin birth was possible.

When Mary greeted her relative, an unusual thing happened. The baby leaped within Elizabeth's womb! We know that by six months a baby is active, but this was a much more violent movement than Elizabeth had experienced before!

The Holy Spirit filled Elizabeth and she began to speak to Mary confirming Gabriel's prediction. She said, "My baby leaped for joy because the mother of my Lord has come to me." God prepared Elizabeth for Mary's unbelievable story. (Mary surely needed someone to believe her!)

A bystander would have been bewildered at this scene and would not have understood the look that passed between the two women. It *would* have been hard to explain!

80

(Surely, Elizabeth must have recounted this incident to her son John many times before he started his ministry in the wilderness.)

Back to Mary. She stayed with Elizabeth for three more months, but left before John was born. How much courage and assurance must have come for Mary, as she daily shared Elizabeth's excitement as her time drew near.

It is time to go home. It won't be long before she is showing that she is carrying a child. It is time to face her parents and Joseph. This is a heavy burden for one to carry, one who is so young and inexperienced and vulnerable.

Joseph was a righteous man, but he does not believe Mary's story. What a thing to say to justify her pregnancy! He will put her away quietly so her disgrace will not be as great. Surely, having her stoned does not cross his mind. He was, however, bound to wonder who the father really was, and if it had happened during her three month visit to her relatives. He certainly *was not going to marry her*, though he would try to be kind and discreet to his indiscreet fiancee. Poor Joseph, to lose his Mary and to lose her in such a degrading manner with such foolish explanations on her young lips.

But an angel appeared to him in a dream, saying, "Joseph, son of David, do not be afraid to take Mary as your wife; for that which has been conceived in her is of the Holy Spirit" (Matthew 1:20). The angel reminded him of the prophecy in Isaiah (7:14) that a virgin would bear a child. "And Joseph arose from his sleep, and did as the angel of the Lord commanded him, and took her as his wife, and kept her a virgin until she gave birth to a Son; and he called His name Jesus" (Matthew 1:24,25). Joseph was God-picked, too!

The second chapter of Luke goes into the most detail about the birth of Jesus. Providence moved Joseph and Mary to Bethlehem for the birth. Bethlehem belonged to Rome at this time, and all former citizens had to return to their native city for census and taxation.

God had planned for Jesus to be born in this city of David, though Jerusalem was also called the city of David. God wanted Him born in the place of the shepherds, for Jesus would be the Good Shepherd. He wanted Him to be born in Bethlehem, which means "house of bread", for He would be the Bread of Life. It was all carefully planned—and foretold.

Mary must have had a terrible trip from Nazareth to Bethlehem, being nine months pregnant. Pictures artists concoct always show Mary riding on a donkey with Joseph walking by her side. Probably that *is* the way it happened, though the Scriptures do not tell us.

There was no room for Jesus from the first! The hotel owner only saw a very pregnant carpenter's wife, not a royal woman bearing the King of Kings. (Won't he be surprised on Judgement Day to find that he turned away Jesus?) If he had only known, he would have given up his own bed and called in the best midwife of the city! Yet, I'm sure Mary was relieved to have a place in the sweet hay to lay down, a place of privacy – if but for the animals.

Evidently, kind Joseph delivered his little virgin with tenderness. The rough hands of the carpenter may have delivered The Carpenter. They wrapped the baby in swaddling clothes, the custom of the times. Mary had packed her suitcase before she left. I wonder if she knew the scripture said Jesus would be born in Bethlehem?

Jesus came to the common man and the common men were first told of His birth. The shepherds were notified first, as they watched their flocks by night. (Lambing was in the spring.) An angel came to them, frightening them terribly, and announcing that the Saviour had been born, who was Christ the Lord! They were to go to the manger to find Him and a multitude of angels joined the spokesman in a glorious chorus of Hosannas!

The shepherds found Him and told their story to the parents. They found Him in a place where they were comfortable. That is where we find Him today. He takes us just as we are and leads us, as a Shepherd, from the stables of sin to a place that He has prepared for us. If we follow Him, we shall not want!

Mary pondered it all in her heart. Mary pondered her lifetime.

The wise men had been following a special star. Again, the pictures portray three wise men, but the Scriptures do not say how many men there were. Probably because three gifts were given, the assumption is made that there were only three wise men. We only know that there were at least two. There could have been twenty. (We'll ask about that someday.)

These men were Gentiles. God had always planned for the day to come for a kingdom that would be international. It was fitting that the Gentiles were there before Jesus began to teach about the approaching of that kingdom. Somehow, these men knew that the King of the Jews would be found by following this special star and they came to worship Him.

When Herod, the king, heard about the coming of the wise men, it scared him. Was this child to be the usurper of his own throne? He called in his Bible students and asked where this king was supposed to be born. They replied, "In Bethlehem of Judea, for so it has been written by the prophet, 'And you, Bethlehem, land of Judah, are by no means least among the leaders of Judah; for out of you shall come forth a ruler, who will shepherd My people Israel' " (Matthew 2:5,6).

The sly one called in the wise men secretly. "Just exactly where did you first see this star? Go and find this king and then tell me where He is, so I can worship Him, too."

Again, tradition has always showed the wise men arriving right after the shepherds, with all of them in the stable together. Yet the Scripture says, "And they came into *the house* and saw the Child with Mary His mother" (Matthew 2:11). They worshipped Him, gave Him their gifts, and returned home another way, as they were warned by a dream not to return to Herod. Do you wonder why Herod had not sent spies behind the wise men? It could be he didn't take much stock in Gentile wise men!

Joseph and Mary take the child away quickly to Egypt, in obedience to an angel's instruction in a dream. They were told that Herod was going to look for the Child, so that he could destroy Him. (The gifts that the wise men had left would now come in handy for money for the trip. God prepares for us before we know we need it.) It had been prophesied that Jesus would be taken to Egypt. "Out of Egypt did I call my Son" (Hosea 11:1).

When wicked Herod realized that he had been tricked by the wise men, he considered the time they had first seen the star. He felt that if all the male children who were two years old and under were killed, he would hear no more of this King of the Jews.

"Where there is jealousy and selfish ambition, there is disorder and every evil thing" (James 3:16). Why should a seventy year old king fear a baby could take his throne?

How our imagination recoils in horror as we see these soldiers, swords dripping blood, going into house after house. How our ears try to shut out the screams of the children and the mothers, and the continued sobbing of those left in the house with the baby growing cold. I wonder how many of those soldiers heard those cries for years afterward, especially the fathers of children! I wonder if any volunteered for such an act of infamy!

Oh, there will be a day of reckoning and every eye will see it!

Herod had not only cleaned out Bethlehem but the environs around it. The mothers would not be comforted. It is one thing to watch a child die of a disease or an accident, but to have it cruelly murdered for no reason would never be forgotten or forgiven!

When Joseph and Mary took Jesus to be circumcized at eight days, a righteous man named Simeon came, in the Spirit, to the temple. He took Jesus in his arms and among the things he said to Mary was, "Behold, this Child is appointed for the fall and rise of many in Israel, and for a sign to be opposed—and a sword will pierce even your own soul..." (Luke 2:34,35). The death of these children was the beginning of the piercing of Mary's heart. She had known many of these toddlers.

Jesus, though a child Himself, had aroused his first martyrs, a band of little boys two years old or younger. When He later said, "For of such is the kingdom of God" as He spoke of little children, did His thoughts go back to that little band of "angels" who died as Herod searched to kill Him?

Joseph had not realized the threat of Herod, but God knew and acted accordingly. What security we have in a God who knows what our enemies are up to!

The next time we meet the family is at Jerusalem at the Feast of the Passover. Jesus is now twelve and old enough to partake of the great annual event. After the days were finished, the caravan started back to Nazareth. They traveled a day before the parents began to realize that they had not seen Jesus.

It was three days later before they found Him! Think how frightened you would be to lose one of your children for so long! To lose Jesus, the Son of God in her care, must have been especially tormenting! She probably knew that He would always be hated by someone! He still is.

Maybe the reason it took so long to find Him was that they were looking in the wrong places. They were looking for a place that would attract a twelve year old boy. They probably first searched among children playing and then places where a child could eat.

But Jesus was with the men—teachers, listening to them and asking questions. It is stated in the King James version as his being with "the doctors." They were astonished at His understanding and His answers. (These doctors must have lived in anticipation for this date all year. Their gathering for the Feast of the Passover was the height of enjoyment and learning.) They were the best, the most knowledgeable, and here was a twelve year old boy holding His own with them! It had never happened before and we can be sure it never happened again!

When Mary saw Jesus she spoke and said just what any other mother would say in like circumstances. "Son why have You treated us this way? Behold, Your father and I have been anxiously looking for You" (Luke 2:48).

Jesus answered, "Why is it that you were looking for me? Did you not know that I had to be in My Father's house? (Luke 2:49). Mary, you of all people should know that my time has come for deeper involvement. I *have* to be about My Father's business. (There comes a time when we who are Christians *must* be about *our* Father's business.)

I heard a learned lady speak some time ago, stating that it has been proven that at this age, a normal twelve year old's brain opens up in a way that it never has before. If this is true, Jesus knew all about it, for He created twelve year old boys.

Jesus went home with them and waited for the time of His ministry to begin. He grew in height, in wisdom, and He pleased both God and men.

The time has come for the great and short work to begin. Jesus and His disciples are invited to a wedding. Evidently Mary had an important part in the preparations.

The wine ran out and she tells him they are out of wine. Jesus said to her, "Woman, what do I have to do with you? My hour has not yet come" (John 2:4).

There have been no miracles up to this point and this is such an odd request to make of the Son of God. Relieve an embarrassed host, a poor host who can't afford more wine.

When Jesus says, "Woman, what do I have to do with you?" it seems to be a rebuke. You are asking for something at the wrong time, and unlike any other miracles that followed.

Mary knew that He *could* do it, but she also knew that the choice was his. Jesus probably wanted her to realize that the family didn't get special privileges. Mary quietly instructed the servants to do anything He requested of them. Six pots of ordinary water were changed to the finest of wines.

Later, another lesson is taught us by Jesus in regard to His earthly family. Jesus has been speaking to the multitudes. His work is going well and He is busy night and day. Mary and her other sons ask to see Him, to interrupt Him. (Mary and Joseph had four sons and some daughters. These sons at this time were unbelievers in the divinity of Jesus. We know that later at least two of the brothers became Christians, James and Jude, for they are authors of two of the books of the New Testament.)

. . . The group stood outside and asked to speak to Jesus. Someone came and told Him and He answered with these profound words. "And stretching out His hand toward His disciples, He said,

'Behold, My mother and My brothers! For whoever does the will of My Father who is in heaven, he is My brother and sister and mother' " (Matthew 12:49,50).

Jesus knew that the familiarity of His earthly family impeded the progress of His work.

> And coming to His home town He began teaching them in their synagogue, so that they became astonished, and said, "Where did this man get this wisdom, and these miraculous powers? Is not this the carpenter's son? Is not His mother called Mary, and His brothers, James and Joseph and Simon and Judas? And His sisters, are they not all with us? Where then did this man get all these things?" And they took offense at Him. But Jesus said to them, "A prophet is not without honor except in his home town, and in his own household."
>
> (Matthew 13:54-57)

It was hard to believe that the "home town boy" whose family they knew well could be The Prophet, the Messiah. Jesus made few converts there.

We meet Mary again, this time at the Cross. The dreadful day is here. The little boy who was spared in Bethlehem is now to die in Jerusalem as the Sacrificial Lamb.

He went through a mock trial in the middle of the night which was unlawful by Jewish decree. What few friends He had in the Sanhedrin probably knew nothing of it.

The Man of Sorrows knew the extent of the cruelty that would encompass. His humanity didn't want to bear the torture any more than we would. He was as divine as His Father but as human as His mother. He prayed for the cup of suffering to pass if possible but for the Father's will to be done. The Father said no to His beloved Son, for there was no other way for us. (Jesus knew this before He came to earth.)

Isaiah, seven hundred years before Jesus was born, had spelled out the degree of degradation and pain that must be borne for God to forgive the sins of the repentant. For He died for us while we were at our worst to help us to become our best, through Him.

" . . . He was despised and forsaken . . . smitten of God and afflicted . . . pierced through . . . crushed . . . scourged . . . carried all men's iniquity . . . silent, like a lamb . . . cut off from the living . . . He was innocent (no violence or deceit) . . . poured out to death . . . numbered with the transgressors . . ." (Isaiah 53).

No other crucified one was so thoroughly and savagely tortured! Anything that could add to His suffering was pursued. They could not find enough to satisfy their taste for blood! "Evil men wax worse and worse."

Mary stood and watched it all. The sword that Simeon had described to her on the day of Jesus' circumcision was piercing her own soul. *She knew who He was.* She didn't know what He would do now. When the crowd jeered Him to come down from His Cross and they would believe; would He come down? She knew He could! Would He who had driven out the moneychangers from the temple allow Himself to be so misused and abused? Did she cry out for vengeance? (We would!)

When He begged for water, He who had the power to turn water into wine, how did she bear them giving Him gall? He asked for so little! And yet *He knew* what they would do. The Word knew the word that had prophesied, "Reproach has broken my heart, and I am so sick. And I looked for sympathy, but there was none, and for comforters, but I found none. They also gave me gall for my food, and for my thirst they gave me vinegar to drink" (Psalm 69:20,21).

The sun deserted the scene! This was fitting. The darkness would help cover His humiliation. He knew God caused it.

Three hours later the greatest of all burdens was laid on Him. The sun came out again and Jesus asked God, "Why, why have You left Me?" Mary saw this new horror and could not understand that the Lamb was bearing all of the black and dirty sins of the whole world. They were all laid at this moment on Him, every sin of all mankind. God, who hates sin (much worse than we do), had to turn away for awhile. Christ paid in His flesh for our iniquities!

Jesus saw even in His intense suffering that Mary and John were there. He said to His mother, "Woman, behold your son!" (John 19:26) Why "woman", not "Mother"? "Mother" would have been a cutting word to she who was already wounded to the heart with grief, perhaps.

The older Son was having to leave His responsibilities and He chose the apostle of love for a substitute. Then He said, "Behold, your mother!" (John 19:27) Now He uses the word, "mother". Don't treat her only as a woman—but as a mother. He gave His human mother to His human servant. "And from that hour the disciple took her into his own household" (John 19:27. She didn't leave the cross without a son. The disciple "whom He loved" would love her as well.

87

How glad we are the story doesn't end here! It doesn't end in despair and failure and horror. FOR HE AROSE! I'm sure Mary wasn't surprised. She knew His work wasn't done.

The last picture that we see of Mary is in the work after the ascension of Jesus to His Home. The eleven apostles and many brethren were meeting in an upper room at Jerusalem. One hundred and twenty of them were meeting and praying for the task ahead. In a few days the kingdom of the Lord would be established in Jerusalem. John was there with Mary, but by now the believing brothers were there, too! (Note Acts 1:14.)

The little boy of Nazareth is only a memory. The carpenter's hands of clay are replaced by the eternal Carpenter who has gone to build us mansions! The voice that stilled the storms now intercedes on our behalf before His Father.

"It is finished" was His final cry on that day of infamy. He wants us to be "fixing our eyes on Jesus, the author and perfector of faith, who for the joy set before Him endured the cross, despising the shame, and has set down at the right hand of the throne of God" (Hebrews 12:2). He wants us, too, to be finished with the carnal life and to put on the new life.

Mary, you did well in carrying out your difficult assignment from beginning to end. God knew you would!

Chapter 13

THE SAMARITAN WOMAN

(John 4:4-42)

"And He had to pass through Samaria." The King James Version says, "And He must needs go through Samaria." Jesus, who had forbade His apostles to teach the Gentiles, had to go through Samaria.

It is true that Samaria was the closest route to Galilee from where He was, but there were probably other reasons why He felt that He needed to go to Samaria.

Hosea tell us in chapter two that the valley of Acher was a "door of hope", and this valley was alongside Samaria. In this same chapter we find this writing, "And I will sow her for Myself in the land. I will also have compassion on her who had not obtained compassion, and I will say to those who were not My people, 'You are My people!' And they will say, 'Thou art my God!'" (Hosea 2:23)

Jesus knew He had something to accomplish in Samaria. He was going to lay a foundation for a future work that would not be built on for at least ten years.

God chose the Jews for His people because they alone remembered Him. The Gentiles forgot Him and worshipped many gods. God gave them up, for awhile.

But He still loved them. He had fashioned them with His own hands just as He had the Jews; it was His hidden plan to bring together in one body all nations. Samaria was part of that plan. So, He went with His apostles to the land despised by all Jews.

He sat down tired, hot, hungry, and thirsty at a famous place, Jacob's well. How many memories must have flooded His heart as

He thought back to the meetings at that well by the patriarchs and their families.

The disciples left Him there alone so that they could go and buy food. It is suggested by the Bible commentator Matthew Henry that, "It would seem that He was but a tender man, and not of robust constitution; it would seem, His disciples were not tired, for they went down into the town without any difficulty, when their Master sat down, and could not go a step further. Bodies of the finest mould are most sensible of fatigue, and can worst bear it."

We do know that Isaiah tells us that He was not of "stately form or majesty that we should look upon Him, nor appearance that we should be attracted to Him" (Isaiah 53:2).

How many times a well was used for a woman to have her life changed by God! We think of Rebecca and Rachel who were in the lineage of Christ, first meeting them at a well. Jesus knew there was going to be another woman's life changed by this providential meeting, but not a woman of the same caliber. Rather, a Samaritan woman.

The Samaritans were part Jew and part Gentile, a mongrel race. The king of Assyria had left the very poorest of Jews behind in that land when he took the Jewish nation captive. They had intermarried with the Gentiles and other Jews came in, who did the same thing. They governed themselves by the five books of Moses and worshipped on Mount Gerizim instead of Jerusalem.

Jesus looked at the woman and made the simplest of requests. "Give me a drink."

She replies, "How come you ask me for a drink since you're a Jew and I'm a Gentile?" She thinks herself to have the advantage. Jesus is hot and thirsty and has no way to get a drink; she alone holds the water-pot and cup. She puts down His request. He is the stranger here in *her* territory. (I think it's interesting to note our Lord endured the same treatment as other men.)

"How is it you ask this of me? I thought we weren't even speaking to each other, let alone to ask a favor of me." Here is a man of the "superior race" condescending to not only a woman, but a *Samaritan* woman!

Jesus lets her know that He is a religious man. "If you knew the gift of God, and who it is who says to you, 'Give Me a drink,' you would have asked Him, and He would have given you living water" (John 4:10). (She would have spoken differently, too!)

Jesus, the Master Teacher, gives us an example of how to start where you are with a stranger and lead to a spiritual conversation. He took her where she was and led her to where He wanted her to be.

She had brought up their racial differences but He doesn't answer back on them. Rather, He responds with the offer of a possibility of a gift from God. All are interested in gifts, especially a God-given gift! He compares the gift He can give to one like she can give. She can give literal water; He can give *living* water. He even hints about His own personality ("and who it is who says to you").

This woman is a unique woman. She has a ready mind and tongue. Little did she know that she had been chosen for this interview! "You're not a greater man than Jacob, are you? Who would claim to be greater than Jacob? In fact, you are standing here thirsty while I hold the means to fill your thirst with cool water on a hot day."

How many times have we childishly thought how much God needs us to make Him happy and deign to do Him favors with our little cup of water when the oceans belong to Him?

There are two conversations going on here at the same time. It reminds one of the time Nicodemus and Jesus were talking. Jesus was speaking of the new birth and Nicodemus was thinking about a physical birth. (Note John 3:3-5.) The Samaritan woman here is talking about the water from the well and He is thinking about the spiritual well in our hearts when we are His obedient children.

He tells her that she will have to daily draw the water from the well but the better well of the heart can continue to be replenished and to bubble up into eternal life.

For the second time, she says, "Sir." "Sir, give me this water, so I will not be thirsty, nor come all the way here to draw" (John 4:15).

We wish we could have seen the expression on her face as she made this request. It probably had a mixture of many emotions: curiosity, doubt, amusement, wonder, and even hope. We all hope for something to make us better, and life easier.

Now it is time to get down to business. "Go, call your husband, and come here" (John 4:16).

"I have no husband." (I imagine she was glad none of her neighbors heard this conversation because of her past. They would have laughed!)

"You have well said, 'I have no husband'; for you have had five husbands, and the one whom you now have is not your husband; this you have said truly" (John 4:17,18).

Jesus is setting up a need now. He is stirring her conscience. He is

91

letting her know that even though He knows her past sins, He still wants to give her a gift from God. He isn't going to turn from her though *He really knows her.* Jesus is more interested in her future than her past.

There is no reason for her to deny the charge or even to give excuses. He understood it all and she knew it. She knew He knew! (He knows us to the same degree.)

She said, "You are a prophet." Then, she immediately brings up what they disagree on in doctrine. "Where are we supposed to worship? Which mountain is best? We worship right here and you Jews say it *has* to be Jerusalem."

Jesus answers, in effect, "It won't be long before the place won't matter. You don't worship correctly now, while the Jews do, but soon all that will be asked of true worshippers is that they worship in spirit and in truth. The location will no longer be of importance. God is looking for people who will worship Him from the heart."

How can she be sure that his new doctrine is true? Where does He get His authority to change the law? Will the Jews go along with the new teaching that the place is unimportant to God? As she looks at Him, already believing He is a prophet, she says, "I know that the Messiah is coming."

Jesus said to her, "I who speak to you am He" (John 4:26).

This is a most unusual conversation. So many of the Jews had wondered if Jesus was the Messiah when they saw Him do the great miracles. He had not told them. He had even time after time cautioned the apostles and those whom He had healed to not tell others of His great power. Yet, here in a short conversation with a woman who has an unfortunate past, He lets her *know* who He is!

Why? Maybe because this was his one-time stop in Samaria in His short ministry. He knew that He would only be there two days and that the church would not include the Gentiles for ten years after it was established. Whatever His reason, we certainly do not question; it. He knew what He was about!

His disciples returned and found Him in earnest dialogue with the woman. They were surprised, but they did not criticize Him or seek for an explanation, though the whole situation was most unusual.

The woman left her water-pot and went into the city. (Maybe that was a kind gesture for the thirsty Jews who might not ask a favor of her, as Jesus had. After all, they were friends of her Friend.) She went to the men of the city, probably to the elders who sat in the gates to decide the business of the day.

Meanwhile, the disciples said, "Rabbi, eat." But Jesus was so excited about His discussion and the foreknowledge of where she had gone and what she would do, He could not eat! He tried to show His disciples that Bible classes are more satisfying than food! "My food is to do the will of Him who sent Me, and to accomplish His work" (John 4:34).

He also wanted them to realize the urgency of the message. "Do you not say, 'There are yet four months, and then comes the harvest'? Behold, I say to you, lift up your eyes, and look on the fields, that they are white for harvest" (John 4:35).

(Are *we* saying there are still four months before we must be putting in our seed or our scythe? Would we be interested in setting up a class with such a much-married woman, who was now living out of wedlock? Jesus was.)

Many believed her when she came running to them and said, "He told me everything I have done." Really, He had stressed with her all the things she should NOT have done. We need to remember that He knows all things that *we* have done and should not have done!

Mankind, sad to say, even good mankind, tends to be harder on one sin than another. We are especially hard on sexual sins of women. We just are! The double standard will always be with us, right or wrong. Jesus was teaching many lessons here; may we have the courage to examine them and take them to heart.

With her sinful past and present, she could still be changed and become a vessel of living water that springs up to eternal life. "Just As I Am Without One Plea" is a song for her and thee and me. An encounter with Jesus can turn us around in the right direction.

We don't know the end of her story. Did she give up marriage for the rest of her life? Unlikely, if she were still a young woman. Did she marry the man she was living with? He might not have even been free, or she might not have wanted him for a husband, especially now.

God does not choose to tell us how her life changed. We are left with the thought that Jesus cared even for the "mongrel race" and picked out a test case that surprises many of us. (Surely, there were many once-married women of Samaria who used that well!)

But He knew *she* would believe Him. She was aware of the coming Messiah. She was interested in the differences in the doctrines of the Jews and Samaritans that worshipped the same God. He knew that she would share her faith. She would be a part of the harvest of souls in Samaria.

We are confident that if she did become a true worshipper of God in spirit and in truth, God would lead her to the right decisions for the rest of her life. We know the "misfit" can become a fitted tool for His service as the wells of living water replenished her heart and mind with the hope of eternal life.

He is the potter. When we willingly surrender our body of clay to His skillful hands, we can be shaped into something beautiful, no matter what our past.

> And from that city many of the Samaritans believed in Him because of the word of the woman who testified, "He told me all things that I have done." So when the Samaritans came to Him, they were asking Him to stay with them; and he stayed there two days. And many more believed because of His word; and they were saying to the woman, "It is no longer because of what you said that we believe, for we have heard for ourselves and know that this One is indeed the Savior of the world."
>
> (John 4:39-42)

Isn't it sad that the "wicked Samaritans" believed, and in His own country He had to leave because of their unbelief? And yet it brings to mind what Paul said, " . . . It was necessary that the word of God should be spoken to you first; since you repudiate it, and judge yourselves unworthy of eternal life, behold, we are turning to the Gentiles" (Acts 13:46).

God's goodness is exemplified in this interview with the Samaritan woman. Heaven came down and touched a heart that wanted to please Him. God still gives the increase! We too often pass by on the other side, for we tend to judge a heart by the outside, while God is looking at the inside.

We still have time, hopefully, to rectify our hearts and let them, too, be filled with wells of water that produce eternal life. Will God choose us as the sanctified, the set apart, to teach Samaritans of our day? If so, they will have to see in our face the reflection of love mirrored from the face of the Beloved before they will be teachable.

"And the Spirit and the bride say, 'Come.' And let the one who hears say, 'Come.' And let the one who is thirsty come; let the one who wishes takes the water of life without cost" (Revelation 22:17).

Jesus wanted her and we should too.

Chaper 14

THE FRUSTRATED COOK

Did He say MARTHA! MARTHA!—or did He say martha, martha? We'll never know (here) will we?

Jesus had a family who loved Him in Bethany. This family consisted of two sisters and a brother: Martha, Mary, and Lazarus. They had a deep mutual love for each other. "Now Jesus loved Martha, and her sister, and Lazarus" (John 11:5). I wonder if there is any significance in Martha's name coming first, aside from her probably being the oldest. He *may* have loved her the best.

Martha was the owner of the house, the hostess, the responsible one. Lazarus lived in Bethany, but not necessarily with his sisters (John 11:2). Jesus knew that He could drop in anytime He chose and stay as long as He pleased. He must have looked forward to his trips to Bethany: to relax with that warm family where He could be comfortable and be Himself.

Mary was probably the younger sister; not as much was expected of her. She was the protected one, the emotional one, the baby sister. Mary was less inhibited than Martha and moved quickly with her moods. (We remember Mary running to Jesus after Lazarus' death when she heard that Jesus had arrived.)

Martha had more control. If she was a widow, she had learned through suffering that life goes on. She had learned to be self-sufficient and to provide for herself and Mary.

Now as they were traveling along, He entered a certain village; and a woman named Martha welcomed Him into her home. And she had a sister called Mary, who moreover was listening to the Lord's word, seated at His feet. But Martha was distracted with all her prepara-

95

tions; and she came up to Him and said, "Lord, do You not care that my sister has left me to do all the serving alone? Then tell her to help me." But the Lord answered and said to her, "Martha, Martha, you are worried about so many things; but only a few things are necessary, really only one, for Mary has chosen the good part, which shall not be taken away from her.

(Luke 10:38-42)

Jesus came to Martha's home alone. I had always thought all the apostles and friends who accompanied Jesus dropped in, perhaps uninvited and unexpected. However, it was just Jesus. This changes the context of the story for me. If Mary had deserted Martha while she was preparing for thirteen hungry men, it might have justified Martha's evident hysteria.

Jesus is relaxing and Mary is sitting at His feet listening to Him. Martha was distracted by all her preparations and she came to Jesus and said, "Tell her to help me."

Martha, you're frustrated and irritated about so many things when only one thing really matters. These precious moments are so few and far between and His time is running out.

Martha had overdone; there isn't a hospitable woman who hasn't made the same mistake. She had more pots and pans that she had hands and she needed help. She needed Mary, but Mary was sitting at His feet as if she intended to stay there.

There are two ways to think about this happening. Let's tell it both ways and someday we will ask which was the closest account of the evening.

The "traditional" way, the way I have always heard this passage taught, would go something like this. Martha is upset. (Unexpected company is just about the worst thing that can happen to most women. When you have time to prepare, then hopefully the house is clean, the beds are changed, the baking is done, and a lovely table is set.) But Martha went to too much trouble. She bit off more than she could chew. It finally came to her that she is in the kitchen alone and to her consternation, she feels Mary is shirking her share of the duties.

"Lord, don't you care about me? Doesn't it bother you that my helper is in there with you and I am about to go berserk out here? You tell her to come in here and help me!"

The Lord rebukes right back, "Martha, Martha, shame, shame! Here you are worried and bothered about a whole lot of things that

96

don't matter. Little Mary is in here where *you* ought to be." So, scolded and chastened, Martha slipped in and sat down and they ate a little cold food before they retired. That *may be* just the way it happened.

Could it have been another way? The account would start out the same. Martha is over-doing for her special guest. (What more honored guest could a lady have? Nothing is too good for Him!) Jesus is a bachelor who doesn't get much home cooking. He is an active young man who is bound to be hungry after so much walking. She started too many pots boiling, too many cakes baking. She wanted her best for Him. Where was the finest table cloth and her choice silver and wouldn't fresh flowers be nice? She is in a dead run, the beans are boiling over and the cake is sticking and the flowers are in disarray and *where is Mary?*

Martha looks in the living room not really expecting to find Mary there, but there she is! She is *sitting* and listening to Jesus like she has forever. Martha has two guests!

She probably wants to be out there too, not missing anything and yet she wants to be preparing this unforgettable meal of love. The fun of preparing the meal has now gone. If Mary would come in and help, they could both sit and listen!

She feels free to go to Him and state her case. Have you ever thought about that? She feels free to tattle on her little sister! Shades of sibling rivalry! (This brings out the rapport that Jesus had with people.) "Make her come in and help me!" (I wonder how many times Jesus, the older brother, had heard similar words at home from His younger brothers and sisters.)

Now the crux of the two interpretations of this beautiful account is, how did He say, "Martha, Martha," and we cannot know. We would have had to have been there to know. It could have well been that He looked at her with amusement and understanding. After all, He knows it all. He knew what was going on in the kitchen. He knew that she loved Him and was proving it by the meal she was preparing – by all the extras she was assembling. He didn't call her out of the kitchen and scold her for her lack of wisdom. No doubt He would have continued to visit Mary as a courteous guest until the meal was served if Martha had not demanded of Him intercession.

"Martha, Martha," think about Him saying it twice; surely that has significance. "Friend, friend," aren't you going to too much trouble? Did He answer with a soft answer to quench her wrath? Martha, can't you simplify this meal and hurry out there and join us so that we can all talk? Mary has realized that the meal is not all that important, or rather that there is something *more* important. The three of them being together.

Hopefully, Martha gets the message. She comes to herself. She sees her own foolishness. He smiles, she softens, she chuckles, Mary's guilt lessens and perhaps she jumps up and helps. Maybe He gets to rest a little and then they all enjoy their feast together.

I hope that is the way it happened but the lesson to be learned from either way of thinking is the same. It really doesn't matter if Jesus scolded or gently chided Martha, for she loved Him to the end and He loved her and her household.

Christian housekeepers of today would do well to give thought to too much serving and too many distractions. Jesus shows us the simple way. Guests do not long remember the menu but rather the warmth or lack of warmth of the home. We can come closer to offending by too much "show" than by too sparse a meal.

Matthew Henry says, "Care is good and duty; cumber is sin and folly." Martha was "cumbered about much serving" (Luke 10:40, KJV). We overwork – "put on the dog."

There are times when we enjoy preparing an elaborate meal. Then there are other times for paper plates and a peanut butter sandwich. There are even times for fasting.

When Jesus walked with two of His disciples on the road to Emmaus after He had been resurrected, He talked with them. They later said, "Didn't our hearts burn within us when He talked with us?" The kind of food and the quantity of it is unimportant when we get a chance to "burn" as we listen to a man of God who moves us. There are seasons when the mundane things of the world are meaningless as we fill our hearts and souls with words that change our lives.

Excuses have been made through the years by some good women who say, "If I had the house you have, or linens, or whatever, I would entertain." No, you wouldn't, dear sister, for God says, "He who is faithful in a very little thing is faithful also in much; and he who is unrighteous in a very little thing is unrighteous also in much" (Luke 16:10).

Jesus wants us to use what we have. He knows just *what* we have because He gave us that much. The everyday food is ample even for company. We probably wouldn't serve fried potatoes, pinto beans, cornbread, and a two-egg cake today because of the starches, but it is still good Texas eating. Or if you are in New England country, a big pot of chowder and crackers, baked beans and brownbread and some grapenut pudding for dessert – that's a good meal, too. It is not what is *in* the plate that matters, but what is *on* the face of the hosts that counts! That takes a long time to learn.

Most important, He wants us to plan our lives so that we are not so busy in food preparation or duties of the house that we cannot drop it all and let our hearts burn within us as we meet Him through the proclaimed Word.

This Martha-story is a priority lesson, a teaching to put first things first, a reminder not to waste precious time in non-essentials. *Too often* we get frustrated or irritated like her and become unlovely people through the stress *we place on ourselves*.

What did He want of Martha? Did He prefer an elaborate meal or an intimate evening with the three of them? *You know*. Mary had chosen the best, but Martha had gotten sidetracked. The Word is given to us to make us perfect – in good working order. I hope that Martha never needed to be taught that lesson again.

We need to be mindful that our houses will burn someday with all their furnishings and food, but the heart that continues to "burn with the desire to listen to Him" will someday sit at the table that He has gone to prepare for those who love Him.

Chapter 15

GOD'S "BAD" GIRLS

Rahab

Rahab was a Gentile harlot. She became part of the lineage of Christ! How could *that* ever happen? A *harlot* related to our Lord?

She lived in Jericho. Joshua, God's servant, had sent two spies to scout out the land before an invasion by the Israelites. God had promised to give His people this land and now they were ready to trust Him and take the land. No doubt the spies had inquired of the local people and found that Rahab had an inn. God's providence sent them to a place where they would be protected.

Rahab had already come to the conclusion that God was not on the side of her peopole and so by faith she protected them. She hid them on the roof of her house under flax. The king sent word to her to deliver the men who were at her house but she bravely disobeyed.

She told the men who came after the spies that indeed they had been there but had left only a short time ago and she didn't know which way they went. The men ran toward the Jordan.

Rahab goes up to the top of the house and talks to the Israelites. "I know that the Lord has given you the land, and that the terror of you has fallen on us, and that all the inhabitants of the land have melted away before you" (Joshua 2:9).

She goes on to rehearse all that they have heard about the power of God going back to the opening of the Red Sea which had occurred forty years before. Then she said, "And when we heard it, our hearts melted and no courage remained in any man any longer because of you; for the Lord your God, He is God in heaven above and on earth beneath" (Joshua 2:11).

What a strange place and a strange mouth to be saying – God rules and He will win! (What a shame that the previous generation of God's people did not have the faith that the harlot possessed!) Rahab's faith is recorded in Hebrews 11, the faith chapter. She is numbered among the faithful with Abraham, Sarah, Jacob, Moses, and many others. Sarah and Rahab, side by side, women of faith.

"By faith Rahab the harlot did not perish along with those who were disobedient, after she had welcomed the spies in peace." (Hebrews 11:31).

Rahab asked the spies if they would repay her kindness by sparing her and her family from death. They agreed. They promised. She let them down by a rope, a scarlet rope, which might have been a token of her trade. They told her to keep that same rope in her window and her house would be saved. "So she sent them away, and they departed; and she tied the scarlet cord in the window" (Joshua 2:21).

Did she doubt that they would deliver her? Could she count herself worthy of such deliverance by God's men? Would she have a hard time convincing the rest of the family to stay in the house and await deliverance?

When they razed the city they raised Rahab's name and buried her bad past. The scarlet cord was not needed. Rahab started over and started as a heroine. Only her family survived and they were in debt to her for their very lives. The Jews admired her for her help.

God's love stories always have a happy ending if He is loved back. "The Lord is righteous in all His ways, and kind in all His deeds. The Lord is near to all who call upon Him, to all who call upon Him in truth. He will fulfill the desire of those who fear Him; He will also hear their cry and will save them. The Lord keeps all who love Him; but all the wicked, He will destroy" (Psalms 145:17-20).

The Lord forgave Rahab. She was no longer a harlot. Her past was forgiven and forgotten. She was justified by her works. She proved her faith by her actions. The Holy Spirit tells us in James 2:25, "And in the same way was not Rahab the harlot also justified by works, when she received the messengers and sent them out another way?"

The last mention we have of Rahab's life is found on the first page of the New Testament. What a tribute it is to a repentant harlot and what a blow to the self-righteous, the super critical, that Rahab is named in the lineage of Christ!

"And to Salmon was born Boaz by Rahab; and to Boaz was born

Obed by Ruth; and to Obed, Jesse; and to Jesse was born David the king" (Matthew 1:5,6).

One of God's bad girls ended right and is given honor to this day. Not many women are named in Matthew's account of the blood-line of Christ. In fact, only five. they were Tamar, who causes a raising of eyebrows, Rahab, the former harlot, Ruth, the foreign Moabitess, Bathsheba, who sinned with David, and little Mary, who was and is often thought a sinner by the unbeliever. We see God turning things upside down again to humble us all. "For everyone who exalts himself shall be humbled, and he who humbles himself shall be exalted" (Luke 14:11).

God has never tolerated sin in man or woman. The wages of sin will ever be death. Yet, God loves the "strange woman" as Solomon called her and He wishes she would turn around in repentance. He knows her past and the circumstances that have led to her downfall. He also know her potential for good.

Jesus put it this way, "Truly I say to you that the tax-gatherers and harlots will get into the kingdom of God before you. For John came to you in the way of righteousness and you did not believe him, but the tax-gatherers and harlots did believe him; and you, seeing this, did not even feel remorse afterward so as to believe him." (Matthew 21:31,32).

Mary Magdalene

Mary Magdalene once had seven demons in her. We don't know how she first contacted the Lord. We don't know her age, only that she was from Magdala near the Sea of Galilee. Jesus cast out her demons. Demons could take people over in that day without their consent. Even children were possessed by cruel demons who would try to destroy the child. Christ gave His apostles power over them.

Probably after the removal of such an evil power, the cleansed one was often branded and avoided. He would be "different", thought peculiar. God teaches his children to call no man common or unclean."

Mary found that Jesus did not turn away from her. We do not know how long she had been possessed and if she had any family left. Even family can turn from a tainted relative.

Mary did not let Jesus go after her cleansing. She decided to ever be with Him. He was not only her friend, but her protector for He understood her. She loved Him.

Many women followed Jesus in Galilee. They ministered to Him. Mary Magdalene was one of them. Wherever Jesus went, she went. No doubt others who had been healed the same way found no place for themselves in society, but were safe with him as well.

> And it came about soon afterwards, that He began going about from one city and village to another, proclaiming and preaching the kingdom of God; and the twelve were with Him, and also some women who had been healed of evil spirits and sicknesses: Mary who was called Magdalene, from whom seven demons had gone out, and Joanna the wife of Chuza, Herod's steward, and Susanna, and many others who were contributing to their support out of their private means.
>
> (Luke 8:1-3)

Jesus set the example of how to treat the unloved and the ones who have a hard time adjusting because of their past. We are told to go out to the highways and the hedges to teach all who will listen, no matter what caste or past. Bring them into the kingdom. Jesus *wants* them and if we are to be like Him we must want them, too.

The time of the crucifixion comes. With what horror Mary Magdalene realizes what they are going to do to the Son of God, her friend! Just as He never deserted her, neither will she desert Him. He could count on her! The apostles fled but she didn't. She was at the cross when the Roman centurion said, "Truly, this man was the Son of God!" (Mark 15:39).

Joseph of Arimathea then wrapped the body of Jesus and placed it in his own tomb. Mary M. sat by the tomb entrance along with another Mary. Someone has written,

> Not she with traitorous kiss her Saviour stung,
> Not she denied Him with unholy tongue –
> But she, while apostles shrank did dangers brave,
> Last at the cross, and first at the grave.
>
> Anon.

On the day of His resurrection, He appeared to her first. Why her? Why not Peter or his beloved John or Mary, His mother? One reason was that she was *there*, waiting for Him. No doubt she had heard Him tell that He would rise again on the third day. Peter gave up on Him and went fishing, but Mary M. didn't. She waited.

"Now after He had risen early on the first day of the week, He first appeared to Mary Magdalene, from whom He had cast out seven demons. She went and reported to those who had been with Him, while they were mourning and weeping. And when they heard that He was alive, and had been seen by her, they refused to believe it" (Mark 16:9).

What did He say to her? What was the expression on her face when she knew that He lived again? That precious meeting was sacred and untold. It belongs to the two of them. (We, too, have our precious meetings with Him, where "He walks with me and He talks with me and He tells me I am His own").

She hastens to the eleven apostles and tells them that He lives, but they don't believe her. What does *she* know!

When Jesus appears to them, He scolds them for their unbelief and hardness of heart. They may have been rude to her, ridiculed her, put her down. Jesus knew their reaction and their hardness of heart. He knows today when we mistreat anyone, especially those who cannot defend themselves and He handles it. He handled it here. To be hard of heart is not to be like Jesus! Jesus loved Mary Magdalene to the end, still loves her. If we cannot love the Marys of the world and especially of the church, we will have to bear our own sin. "If you are wise, you are wise for yourself, and if you scoff, you alone will bear it" (Proverbs 9:12).

God is not partial, nor is His Son. When we show partiality, we sin. Peter once said after a lesson given to him by God, ". . . I most certainly understand now that God is not one to show partiality, but in every nation the man who fears Him and does what is right is welcome to Him" (Acts 10:34,35).

And James, the Lord's brother, caps it all when he says by inspiration, "But if you show partiality, you are committing sin and are convicted by the law as transgressors" (James 2:9).

When a sinner repents, the angels rejoice. If *we* can't rejoice, we have a serious problem, we have "heart trouble!" There are no "second class citizens" in the kingdom of God, second class because of their past. Mary Magdalene helped prove that.

For She Loved Much
(Luke 7:36-50)

Jesus got a dinner invitation from a Pharisee which He accepted. A single man who "had no place to lay His head" could anticipate a fine meal. He *should* have been honored as a special guest. If that Pharisee had known he was entertaining the Son of God, Jesus would have received different treatment. An honored guest would have been greeted with a kiss from the host. The servant would have washed his feet and rubbed his hair with oil. Jesus was not extended any of these courtesies. This was just a curious host. Who was this man? How could He do such miracles? Where did He come from and what was His mission? Should He be taken seriously?

Perhaps the Pharisee wanted to know more about the kingdom that Jesus and His apostles were teaching about. Many selfish and greedy Pharisees had tried to force John to baptize them so they could be in on the ground floor of the coming kingdom. (How they longed for the return of all the splendor of a kingdom like Solomon's and to be rid of the rule of the cruel Romans!)

Jesus knew that he was not an important guest to the host and that the customs of the day had been ignored. No kiss was given; his feet remained unwashed. His hair was not smoothed or oiled and no special attention had been given to Him. Of course Jesus made no demands of his host but allowed the humiliation.

As He lay at the table, a woman came up behind Him and stood at His feet, crying. Her tears fell on His unwashed feet and she had no towel to wipe them away. She unloosened her long hair quickly and wiped his feet with her hair. A shocking act! Since Jesus did not rebuff her, she became braver and kissed His feet and put perfume on them.

Maybe she had been following Him for some time, hoping for an opportunity to anoint Him in this way. Yet, how did she *dare* walk, uninvited, into a wealthy Pharisee's home? She was not only uninvited, but unwelcome, for she was a noted sinner. But she had a compulsion, maybe an obsession, to touch Him, to serve Him, to give Him a gift. She hadn't rushed in, pushed her way, and knelt before Him in haste and foolishness. Rather, she went behind Him, quietly, faceless, nameless, just wanting to touch Him. (Wouldn't *you* have liked to touch Him?) Her heart was full of love and her eyes full of tears. There were many tears, enough to fall on His feet and to be wiped away. She stood there for awhile to see how He would react, but He showed no reaction. If He had been impatient with her, surely she would have run. If He had pulled her around in front of Him and seated her, then He would have insulted His host by forcing an uninvited guest, one the host did not want in his house.

His wet feet embarrassed her. She hastily used the only thing she had to dry them, her hair. She kept crying and wiping His feet and He still made no move or showed any displeasure. She thought herself to be accepted by Him, which she was. She dared to stay longer, so she rubbed his feet with the perfume. (Jesus later on gave the example to His apostles that they should not think themselves too good to wash feet, or any other job that needed to be done. He didn't have to teach this lesson to her, for she was already a "foot-washer".)

The host is watching this scene with interest. How will Jesus handle this bad woman? The Pharisee doesn't cast her out or scold her. Evidently, he feels that it is up to Jesus to handle it. Have you ever thought how most men would react in such a situation?

It seems to me that the average man would be a little, if not a lot, embarrassed. Here He is a tolerated guest and an uninvited woman is crying, sniffing, her hair all undone, wiping Jesus' feet, and then continuing her stay by applying perfume to His feet. She isn't leaving. Most men, even if they liked the attention, would probably say, "Not now, your timing is off. Thank you very much, but no, thank you." What makes the situation even harder for a man is that there were other guests watching the whole event. It appears that the next move *has* to be up to Jesus.

The host might have watched in amusement and bored sophistication. We know what he was thinking, for God reveals it. "If this man were a prophet He would know who and what sort of person this woman is who is touching Him, that she is a sinner" (Luke 7:39). "*If* this man were a prophet" is in his mind. You can see the rest of that thought would be, "but He is not a prophet. If He were a prophet, He would know who she was without even looking around at her. He would *know* she was a sinner."

Jesus took the lead. "Simon, I have something to say to you."
"Say it, Teacher."

Jesus gave a parable. Parables are easier to get a point across. The parable went like this: If two men owed a debt and they could not pay and were forgiven that debt, which one would love the most–the one who had been forgiven a hundred denarii or the one who had been forgiven fifty denarii? Simon answered that it would be the one who was forgiven more. The bigger debtor would love more. Jesus said, "You're right."

Simon, you are less a debtor than she. (It was hard for a Pharisee to see that he was a debtor at all!) He wanted to call the righteous to repentance, not the sinner. He wanted to choose who got into the kingdom that was coming. He didn't know yet that Christ's kingdom would be very expensive, paid for by His blood.

Then, for the first time, Jesus looked at the woman. His eyes were kind and understanding. *People were not afraid to touch Jesus.* He was so touchable! As He looked at her, He talked to Simon.

"Do you see this woman? I entered your house; you gave Me no water for My feet, but she has wet My feet with her tears, and wiped them with her hair. You gave Me no kiss; but she, since the time I came in, has not ceased to kiss My feet. You did not annoint My head with oil, but she annointed My feet with perfume" (Luke 7:44-46).

What a vindication! What a championing of her! What acceptance! Jesus is not on the defensive but rather the host is. She passed and he failed! *What strength Jesus had.* And why not — didn't He create the world and Simon as well?

He could endure the embarrassment of the situation, if He was embarrassed, which I seriously doubt. He was not going to allow this woman to be hurt by a self-righteous Pharisee. He shows us over and over that we can count on Him when we are reaching for Him! He shows us that He is more than a man, that indeed, He is the Son of God! We can let our weight down and trust in the arms that are strong to defend us!

If He had stopped here, He would have righted the occasion and would have done more than was expected by Simon or the woman, but He does not stop.

"For this reason I say to you, her sins, which are many, have been forgiven, for she loved much; but he who is forgiven little, loves little. And He said to her, 'Your sins have been forgiven' " (Luke 7:47,48).

The heart of the whole story is in this last paragraph. Those who are forgiven much usually love much. The worse the sinner, the deeper their love for God after repentance. The less the sinner, too often, the less the love for God. Usually, the ones in the church that you can count on to serve *in any way* are those who have been forgiven more and know it. These are the foot-washers.

Jesus speaks to the woman for the first time. He has only looked at her before now. "Your sins have been forgiven." Don't you know you are clean? Don't you know I love you? The kingdom is going to be made up of people like you and few of the Pharisees will find it. (Few of them find it today.)

His parting words were, "Your faith has saved you; go in peace" (Luke 7:50). Dry those tears. Start again. Put your hand in Mine and I'll help you.

I have seen the love for Him in some of His former "bad girls". How they love and how they grow and change!

We need to constantly examine *our* attitudes and feelings for them. Do we keep them "different" or do we love them with an unpretended love. Are they family? If we cannot accept and forgive and love all of God's children here, then we well may not get to enjoy heaven with them there. Their great love for Him is their anchor.

The last thing He said to her was, "Go in peace." The balm of Gilead was applied to her heart. Scars were left – but only scars. Her tears are dried and the long hair is back in place.

Caught in the Act
(John 8:3-7)

This is one of the tenderest, most touching stories in the whole Bible. If you can throw your imagination into force and let yourself become the woman caught in adultery, you will find a fresh understanding of the whole account.

The enemy of Christ had another test with which to entrap Him. It *was* a clever one! They thought they had Him no matter how He answered. They had spent hours setting this delicious net and this one was fool-proof. Yes, the scribes and the Pharisees had done their best and this time there would be no failure!

It is credible to believe that they set the trap by sending the man to the adulteress, though we do not know this to be true. We *do* know that the man was not arrested, only the woman. When they brought her to Him as He was teaching, interrupting a Bible class, they said, "We caught this woman in the very act." If they caught the woman in the act, then they *knew* who the man was. The law said that both should be stoned. They were not interested in a double-stoning, but in a single "hanging."

A woman caught in the act. She knew the penalty if she were caught by more than one witness. No doubt she thought herself alone with the man. Suddenly there was a crowd grabbing her and pushing her out of the rendezvous. Her clothes were in disarray, what clothes she had or could grab. There were too many to resist and her legs must have turned to rubber as they pushed her toward sure death. These men were the "good men", the law keepers; what chance did she have for mercy?

109

Where are they taking her? The noise must have attracted other bystanders and they joined the crowd. She finally knew that they were heading for the temple. There would be no chance for her now. The temple represented the law and the law said that she must die by stoning. There is no need to resist. "And they set her in the midst." They *set* her, placed her firmly, in the middle of the group.

She was no stranger, she knew them and they her. Righteous indignation flashed from the eyes of the unrighteous men!

"Teacher, (they had called him "deceiver" the day before) we caught her in the act and Moses says, 'Stone her.' What do *you* say?"

This was going to be good, for there is *no way* for Him to answer right. If He says to stone her, He breaks the Roman rule commanding Jews not to administer capital punishment. Also, He would be unmerciful toward her. *He* won't want to stone her! If he says *not* to stone her, He will be breaking Moses' law. There will be witnesses that He is a lawbreaker and deserves death. Speak up and hang yourself, Jesus of Nazareth.

We noted in the previous story that Jesus does not allow Himself to be on the defensive. He knows what to say and when to say it. Jesus did not even look at the trembling woman. (There were enough eyes on her.) He just stooped down and began writing on the ground with His finger. No one knows what He wrote. He didn't have to meet their demands of an instant response. He took time to let the situation simmer.

They persisted in asking Him. They had gone to too much trouble to let this trap go untriggered. They had too much at stake. The woman was unimportant and her death meant nothing to them. She was just the bait.

Jesus straightened up, stood up, and looked at them, unafraid. What did He see? How often His heart must have broken for the evil he saw in the faces of those who should have been the most righteous. Jesus, however, was a realist and He knew what was in the heart of man.

Eagerly they waited for what He would say. He had only two choices: stone her or not stone her. He said, in effect, to stone her (keep the law). Those of the group who are without sin; *you* stone her. Now, who was on the defensive?

The crowd was made up of both old and young men. Older men ought to be wiser men and in this crowd the older men left first. They just quietly were no longer part of the scene. No speeches, no threats, no grumbling, they just left. When the old were gone the young men stood alone and they, too, began to disperse. The force of the crowd was gone as the individual responded to his own guilt.

The story isn't over. She is still there. Jesus began writing again on the ground. Jesus writes and she waits. Why doesn't she run? This is her first chance to escape! How can she *not* run?

I guess you don't react as usual after an encounter with Jesus. He had saved her life. The enemies were gone and He was her Deliverer.

Jesus stood up again and this time He looked at her. What did He see? He saw a woman fashioned by the hands of God. He saw a beautiful woman, probably, who had gone astray. He saw a shipwrecked life and He knew the unhappiness that was hers, for the "way of the transgressor is hard".

"Woman, where are they?" Where is that crowd of violent men with stones in their hands? Where is that group of "righteous" men who would love to kill a woman for the sins of the flesh, but could not because of the memory of their own? Wasn't there even *one* who could throw that first stone, who could condemn?

"No one, Lord." She stayed. It had not all been said—yet. What do I do now? How do I rebuild? How do I pick up the pieces?

"And Jesus said, 'Neither do I condemn you; go your way. From now on sin no more" (John 8:11). Go back to life, but to a better life. You have another chance. You do not need to be an adulteress; that way nearly cost you your life. But the choice is yours.

I wonder what choice she made. It is possible she might have joined the women who followed Jesus. She would have been accepted in that group. She may have gone home to a husband and family. She may have grown up in those few minutes.

Forgiven lady, what *did you do* with Jesus?

Chapter 16

THE TEN TALENT WOMAN

And to one he gave five talents, to another, two, and to another, one, each according to his own ability; and he went on his journey. . . Now after a long time the master of those slaves came and settled accounts with them. And the one who had received the five talents came up and brought five more talents, saying, 'Master, you entrusted five talents to me; see, I have gained five more talents.' His master said to him, 'Well done, good and faithful slave' . . .

(Matthew 25:15,19,20,21)

All of us have God-given talents. Each of us are required to increase our talents by use. Male and female will answer for their neglect of honing and perfecting their talents, their gifts.

". . .And from everyone who has been given much shall much be required; and to whom they entrusted much, of him they will ask all the more" (Luke 12:48). God asks more of the five talented person and so does mankind. We will be judged by our abilities, potentialities, and opportunities.

People differ; even identical twins are not identical in soul and spirit. There are all sorts of combinations of temperaments in each of us. We are like snowflakes, each flake different from another. And "different" as we are, we marry someone who is "different", too.

There are married hares and tortoises, sly foxes and meek lambs. lions and mice, and oxen and mules, etc. etc. etc. The fast and the slow, the wise and foolish, the organized and nonplanner, the lazy and the energetic marry each other. Ideally, the man is the ag-

113

gressor, the planner, the intellectual breadwinner married to the less aggressive, not-so-organized, slower moving wife and mother.

However, the longer we live, the more we observe that man turns many things upside down and God has the *power* to make them work upside down. Glory can come to Him in any situation and seldom are many situations ideal!

He reminds us that "the race is not to the swift" (Ecclesiastes 9:11). It is not how fast we ran, but how well, and most important – did we finish the race? Someone has wisely said, "God will not look you over for medals, degrees, or diplomas, but for scars."

Inspiration introduces a married couple named Aquila and Priscilla. They seem to be one of these "upside-down" couples, for we find her named first more often than her husband. Priscilla was a "ten-talent" woman. She gave her all and was blessed with a husband who loved God and her.

To my knowledge, there are few women's names who are placed before the man's name in the Bible. Miriam, Mary, and Priscilla are some of these. Miriam's name was place first because she was the leader in a mini-rebellion. The other two were not out of their rightful place as God's servants, but were shown special honor.

"Then Miriam and Aaron spoke against Moses because of the Cushite woman whom he had married" (Numbers 12:1). Their enmity toward her fostered them to question Moses' God-given leadership. "And they said. . .'Has He not spoken through us as well?' " (Numbers 12:2).

No, he had not spoken to them as well. Moses did not try to reason with them or defend himself for "the man Moses was very humble, more than any man who was on the face of the earth" (Numbers 12:3).

Suddenly, God said to Moses, Aaron, and Miriam, "You three come out to the tent of the meeting." (Can you imagine how you would feel if God said that to you?) Miriam didn't seem worried. She wasn't scared to face God! But God verified Moses and then closed with these words, "Why then were you not afraid to speak against My servant, against Moses?" (Numbers 12:8). God's anger burned. When the cloud lifted there stood Miriam, white as snow with leprosy. Her brothers interceded for her, but God required her to stay outside the camp for seven days, though she was healed. (I don't want my name placed first as Miriam's. Do you?)

Mary, the mother of Jesus, had her name placed first once. "And they came in haste and found their way to Mary and Joseph, and the baby as He lay in the manger" (Luke 2:16). Mary was not seeking preeminence but God chose to place her name first in this instance. It is easy to understand that Mary was a chosen one. She was the virgin picked to be the earthly mother of Jesus, our Lord. Joseph was the head of his house and his name is used first on other occasions but he was not the father of Mary's first baby! God showed this by His naming Mary first on this occasion.

Priscilla is the last of the three whose name was placed first. Her husband, Aquila, was always mentioned first when it was proper to acknowledge him as the head of the house. She was named first at times, probably because of her zeal and her service and wisdom.

Commentator Matthew Henry says of her, "And doubtless it had a good influence upon this that Priscilla the good wife of the family was so very eminent and forward in religion, so eminent that she is often named first. A virtuous woman that looks well to the way of her household, may do much toward the advancement of religion in a family. When Priscilla and Aquila were at Ephesus though but sojourners there, yet there also they had a church in their house."

Paul met this couple in Corinth and he joined them in tentmaking. "And he (Paul) found a certain Jew named Aquila, a native of Pontus, having recently come from Italy with his wife Priscilla, because Claudius had commanded all the Jews to leave Rome. He came to them, and because he was of the same trade, he stayed with them and they were working; for by trade they were tentmakers" (Acts 18:2,3). They became among Paul's dearest and beloved friends.

Later, the three of them traveled to Cenchrea where Paul keeps a vow. Here Priscilla's name is first. . . "And with him were Priscilla and Aquila. In Cenchrea he had his hair cut, for he was keeping a vow" (Acts 18:18). Did she suggest the vow or help to sustain him during the vow? Could be either or both.

Paul leaves them at Ephesus and goes on to Antioch. They heard an eloquent preacher named Apollos. He was not only eloquent but he was "mighty in the Scriptures." He spoke accurately the things concerning Jesus but was inaccurate about baptism. He did not realize that John's baptism was taken out of the way when Christ died and the church established. He was teaching an outdated baptism unknowingly.

Priscilla and Acquila took him aside (probably home with them) and "explained to him the way of God more accurately" (Acts 18:26). You can hear Priscilla saying, "Let's take him home and get this matter straight." If she had just thought about it, but had waited for her husband to act on it, Apollos might have had to wait for others to instruct him. Souls could have been lost in the interim. They would have been lost by an eloquent, inaccurate teacher.

Every sincere Bible student should have the attitude of fact-finding, no matter whose mouth is used to impart knowledge. Priscilla didn't jump up while Apollos was preaching and shame or humiliate him. Rather, the teaching team, one in Christ, took him to themselves. They carefully and wisely led Apollos to a better understanding of the Word. They used their talents. "And he began to speak out boldly in the synagogue. But when Priscilla and Aquila heard him, they took him aside and explained to him the way of God more accurately" (Acts 18:26).

The church met in their house often. This takes a lot of giving from the lady of the house. *You could count on Priscilla!* In fact, you could count on Priscilla and Aquila to die for right, to risk their very lives. Paul said, "Greet Prisca and Aquila, my fellow workers in Christ Jesus, who for my life risked their own necks, to whom not only do I give thanks, but also all the churches of the Gentiles; also greet the church that is in their house" (Romans 16:3-5).

Prisca, we would love to know just what happened when you risked you life for Paul. Did you think of the plan? Did you, like Rahab, send the enemy in another direction? *Whatever* happened, it worked, and Paul was saved. Priscilla was using her talents, her wits, her bravery for the good of God's chosen apostle, Paul, and Aquila did the same.

This married couple "exposed their necks" to deliver Paul. They laid their lives on the line. What a pair! Does it really matter which one of them thought of how to save Paul? Would people like this be involved with petty thinking, competition, or a desire for personal glory? No way.

The next time we hear them spoken of is when they send their greeting and fittingly it is said, "Aquila and Prisca greet you heartily in the Lord, with the church that is in their house" (1 Corinthians 16:19).

The last mention of them is found in 2 Timothy 4:19, close to the end of Paul's life. "Greet Prisca and Aquila. . ." Paul said this to his beloved Timothy. Prisca came to his mind and his pen first. If we had known her we would have understood this. God just tells it as it is.

God still has his Priscillas. The present Priscillas are thankful for that pace-setter of long ago. God has placed on many good women abilities and responsibilties that He expects to be used. "Use it or lose it" has always been a warning from God. However, discretion must be an important characteristic of every godly woman. No matter how talented a woman is, she still has God-given restrictions. The pulpit will never be hers but teaching and good works must be. She will always be the "lesser light" in public service, but *real* Priscillas could care less! There is much to do and so little time to do it that we cannot chafe about what is *not* ours to do.

If we could have talked with her centuries ago and could have asked her if she felt "put down" or slighted because she could not be a preacher or an apostle, I'm sure she would have laughed. Here was a fulfilled woman busy working with her husband and Paul making tents, a church in her house wherever she lived, a woman so involved that she risked her neck, and a woman who often sends cheerful greetings to other Christians. What did she lack? Nothing! What did she gain? Everything! She found a place to use all of her talents, to double and even redouble her gifts. She found her niche!

Not all Priscillas are as fortunate in having an Aquila. His ego was big enough to handle his wife's good works. He *was* a big man! Aren't we glad that she was not married to Ananias, the greedy thief, or Demas, the preacher whose heart was in Thessolonica, or Alexander, the big-mouth, or prideful Diotrophes?

Surely God is mindful of whom to put together! He must often draw Aquilas to Priscillas. I've met quite a few of those couples, those special men and women. God bless them!

Ten-talented women must not have a spirit of fear for that is not God-given. "For God has not given us a spirit of timidity, but of power and love and discipline" (2 Timothy 1:7). Satan wants to defeat us and to make us afraid. He is a skillful discourager. God is greater than Satan and He gives us power to overcome the wicked one.

If perchance a Priscilla of today is reading this book and knows that she is married to a man who despises her talents and would have her live an unfruitful life, what then? *Only God's power and wisdom can solve this problem!* First, there is going to have to be a lot of time spent in prayer. Prayer for daily wisdom, prayer for God to open the heart of the husband, prayer for the right attitude toward the husband, and prayer for patience and ability to wait on the Lord.

Her talents will never justify the neglect of her husband, her head, or her reverence and respect for him and his authority! Her talents will never justify her shaming him or embarrassing him in a willful manner! His needs *must* be supplied for her to please God. Her unusual gifts do no negate the priorities of a clean house, good meals at the right time, clean clothes, and a security to him of her "being there."

However, God does not require for her to "be there" when her menial chores are done. There is time, in time, for good work in the home and for good works outside of the home. God's wisdom will enable her to set up the proper schedule.

Pre-school children take about all the time there is, but they don't stay that age very long. God tells us to "redeem the time" or "buy up the time." Our homes can be used for headquarters for learning and growing until we can be free to serve God outside the home. Young married women are commanded to be home with their children if at all possible (1 Timothy 5:14; Titus 2:4-5).

In the parable we began with, the one-talent man was fearful so he hid his talent and was lost for it. The five-talent woman's heart will burn within her if she has to hide her talent and she, too, will be lost if she does so. She *must* use what she has and double what she has been given for the peace of her own soul!

God will give her wisdom if she asks for it. She, too, can stay her husband's helper as she develops and strengthens her abilities to serve God. Her husband should always be confident that she is on his side and that he can safely trust that she will "do him good all the days of her life."

No matter what the temperaments of each Christian couple, they must be used for the spread of the kingdom. We must "work. . .as long as it is day; night is coming, when no man can work" (John 9:4). The reapers are few and the harvest is white. Grab a scythe and work together to the best of your ability and time, reaping together as a team, hopefully, or reaping alone. . .if need be.

Chapter 17

THE
SINGLE WOMAN

Many women will read this chapter first, single women, mothers of, and concerned friends. What to do, what to do, is the question that consumes many single women. The pressures of being unmarried are great in our two-by-two society!

In the past, it was a universal expectation that all women must marry or be branded old maids. This is no longer so. Many women choose careers and the single life. Many women feel freer to choose thus; this could be good.

To be married or to remain single should be the choice of each person. A lifelong commitment should be made only by two committed persons, committed to each other—and to God. To marry because of outside pressures or to please parents or conform to society's demands often results in an unhappy life. Not only for the woman, but for the mate and the offspring.

What does God say about this subject? "It is good for a man not to touch a woman" (1 Corinthians 7:1). It is good to live a celibate life. "Yet I wish that all men were even as I myself am" (1 Corinthians 7:7). What *was* Paul? A "eunuch", by choice. (See Matthew 19:12)

"But I say to the unmarried and to widows that it is good for them if they remain even as I" (1 Corinthians 7:8). It is good if they choose to live without sexual fulfillment.

Did Paul have a right to marry? Oh, yes. "Do we (Paul and Barnabas) *not have a right* to take along a believing wife, even as the rest of the apostles, and the brothers of the Lord and Cephas (Peter)?" (1 Corinthians 9:5).

Well, why *didn't* you marry, Paul? He didn't choose the encumbrance. "For if I preach the gospel, I have nothing to boast of, for I am under compulsion; for woe is me if I do not preach the gospel. For I do this voluntarily, I have a reward; but if against my will, I have a stewardship entrusted to me. What then is my reward? That, when I preach the gospel, I may offer the gospel *without* charge, so as not to make full use *of my right* in the gospel" (1 Corinthians 9:16,17). Marriage was one of the rights that Paul gave up.

Paul as a single man could live more cheaply and travel more extensively than if he were a married man and a father. Paul always felt himslf "chiefest of sinners" because of his former persecution of the church. He wanted to give all and he wanted to encourage everyone else to give all.

There are men like this today, and there are women who want to give all to God as well. There are women whose hearts burn to serve God and who do not wish to be married. They, too, do not choose to be encumbered.

Paul spells this out, "But I want you to be free from concern. One who is married is concerned about the things of the world, how he may please his wife, and his interests are divided. And the woman who is unmarried, and the virgin, is concerned about the things of the Lord, that she may be holy both in body and spirit; but one who is married is concerned about the things of the world, how she may please her husband. And I say for your own benefit; not to put a restraint upon you, but to promote what is seemly, and to secure undistracted devotion to the Lord" (1 Corinthians 7:32-35).

He knew that the majority of people need to be married. "But because of immoralities, let each man have his own wife, and let each woman have her own husband" (1 Corinthians 7:2).

God has special work for special women. The world is divided into male and female. The female can go into places to do works for other women where men cannot go. *There is a need!* Jesus took many women with Him on His journeys, some were married and some were not. "And it came about soon afterwards, that He began going about from one city and village to another, proclaiming and preaching the kingdom of God; and the twelve were with Him, and also some women who had been healed of evil spirits and sicknesses: Mary who was called Magdalene, from whom seven demons had gone out, and Joanna the wife of Chuza, Herod's steward, and Susanna, and many others who were contributing to their support out of their private means" (Luke 8:1-3).

Women helped Paul as he went into the world and worked side by side with him. "Indeed, true comrade, I ask you also to help these

women who have shared my struggle in the cause of the gospel. . ."
(Philippians 4:3).

Christian colleges are beginning to encourage the sending of young women into all the world on campaigns and various works of the Lord. Nothing is more effective in going into all the world and staying there than going in the first place and seeing the need. As the old song says, "Let your eyes see the need of workers today."

Christian families are beginning to finance the work of daughters who want to give themselves to the interests of God. Sometimes, these daughters marry in their mission field. "But if you should marry, you have not sinned; and if a virgin should marry, she has not sinned. Yet such will have trouble in this life, and I am trying to spare you" (1 Corinthians 7:28).

Let's talk about some of those "troubles in this life". It is interesting that this particular instruction is given only to women, virgins. What trouble do married women have that married men do not? It could be sexual. Married life stirs up emotions that would have lain dormant if there had not been a marriage.

The reference for the word "trouble" is also called "tribulation in the flesh". When a man sets the pace the wife tries to keep up, and being the weaker vessel, often she cannot. If she is single, she can better set her own speed. She can rest when she needs to; even retire at an earlier time. She can give quality time if not quantity.

The very role of submission puts a constant God-ordained charge upon her in all her activities and wishes. But one who is married is concerned with how she might please her husband. The "divided interests" are faced each day. Man does not have the submissive role, though all Christians are to live peaceably and to submit to one another.

There is the "trouble" of a family; there are women who could not endure the constant demands of a family. It would be too much. Not all women are meant to be mothers. You will notice even in little girls those who run to play with the babies and those who do not like babysitting. The constant pulling and tugging of little ones can be a mental strain as well as a physical one. We should count the cost of motherhood before we marry.

It would be sad if we could know how many good women throughout the ages have married and conformed to a life for which they were not suited just because they did not understand God's teachings on the advantages of single life. "You do err not knowing the scriptures" (Matthew 22:29 KJ) is still as true today as when it

121

was first spoken by the Lord. The single life has its advantages and disadvantages. One of the disadvantages is pointed out in 1 Corinthians 7:36-38. "But if any man thinks that he is acting unbecomingly toward his virgin daughter, if she should be of full age, and if it must be so, let him do what he wishes, he does not sin; let her marry."

What *does* the older Christian woman who is single do about her support? God's answer found in this reading is that the father provides for the daughter's old age. If she chooses to marry then (probably for companionship and physical care), let her marry. It would be for her security, but if the father wants to continue to care for his daughter all her life and has the means to do it, the daughter would do well to remain single. It would not be wrong for her to marry, but it would be better to stay single. In these days of insurance, godly fathers are blessed in having a way to provide adequately for their single daughters even after their own demise.

We have two examples of women in the New Testament who were self sufficient women with no mention of a husband. Lydia was a seller of purple (an expensive dye used only by the rich). Lydia had her own household, her own home, and she was a devout Jewish woman. Paul converted her, baptized her and her household. She invited Paul and his companions to stay at her home. (Acts 16:13-15).

Phoebe was a servant of the church at Cenchrea. She traveled some, for we see her not only at Cenchrea but at Rome. She was a worthy woman and well thought of by the Christians who knew her. "I commend to you our sister Phoebe, who is a servant of the church which is at Cenchrea; that you receive her in the Lord in a manner worthy of the saints, and that you help her in whatever matter she may have need of you; for she herself has also been a helper of many, and of myself as well (Romans 16:1,2).

In conclusion, this verse comes to mind, "Delight yourself in the Lord; and He will give you the desires of your heart" (Psalms 37:4). If you are single by choice and wish to remain so, you may find comfort in these words. Do not feel guilty or let someone lay guilt on you. Find your own niche. Be single and enjoy it! Dare to be Daniel's sister!

If you are not single by choice and you would choose the married life with all its blessings – and troubles, God will give you the desire of your heart, if it is His will and for your good.

Marriage is a yoke; most of us choose that yoke. However, there are many who blind themselves to the chafing of the yoke, seeing only the garlands wrapped around it. They want the wedding bells, the music, the festivities, the rice and the honeymoon. But they don't want the permanent hitching together for the long haul. It takes a long time for the yoke to wear down smoothly!

Is marriage for you? Take your time. As the song goes, "Married you can always get".

Chapter 18

WHO'S BOSS?

"Everyone wants to be the chief, but no one wants to be the Indian" is an old but true saying. All want to lead but no one wants to follow. The natural man often hates authority.

Discipline is learned. "For the commandment is a lamp, and the teaching is light; and reproofs for discipline are the way of life" (Proverbs 6:23). We are disciplined daily by what we serve. The choice is ours. We can choose a well-ordered life by following God and reaping the happiness thereof, or we can follow the natural inclinations, serve Satan, and reap the unhappiness that is inevitable.

Mankind cannot escape some discipline no matter how he tries. The child is under the authority of his parents. Hopefully, he is loved, trained, protected and supervised, and becomes a good citizen. Woe to the home that allows the child to lead and the parents to follow that lead. No one will prosper or be happy!

The fortunate child is taught to recognize and respect the authority of the teacher and the principal. Too often today we see the child administering the discipline to a cowering teacher. Statistics of teacher abuse are unbelievable! Parents often uphold the undisciplined child no matter what he has done while good teachers are leaving the profession by droves. They know there is no teaching without discipline.

God authorizes governments for the good of man. Chaos always exists where there are no rulers. "Let every person be in subjection to the governing authorities. For there is no authority except from God, and those which exist are established by God" (Romans 13:1). Governments are expected to punish the wrongdoers and to protect our rights. By keeping order they please God, though they may not recognize Him as God. When the people take over and riot goes unchecked, that nation cannot stand. When murderers, rapists, thieves, and whatever are allowed to go unpunished or insufficiently punished, then governments are failing God in His plan for discipline.

> For rulers are not a cause of fear for good behavior, but for evil. Do you want to have no fear of authority? Do what is good, and you will have praise from the same; for it is a minister of God to you for good. But if you do what is evil, be afraid; for it does not bear the sword for nothing; for it is a minister of God, an avenger who brings wrath upon the one who practices evil.
>
> (Romans 13:3,4)

We even find discipline in social relationships. We arrive at the acceptable time, we dress in the expected way, we chew with our mouths closed, and we talk of things that are permitted in our group. The renegade, barefooted and unkempt, foul-mouthed and ill-clothed, bears the cost of non-conformity. The rebel, the undisciplined, do not find the fulfillment God meant for them to have. "Stern discipline is for him who forsakes the way; he who hates reproof will die" (Proverbs 15:10).

God does not suffer rebellion! The rebel always pays—and pays. Conformity has its lasting rewards and rebellion has only a temporary satisfaction. The undisciplined eventually asks for help from the disciplined. The lawless yells for his "rights" which are supplied by the law-keeper. "Poverty and shame will come to him who neglects discipline" (Proverbs 13:18).

The improperly raised child turns into a misfit. He never finds his niche. The impudent comes out of school ignorant and unlearned, unfit to make a living or to find a place in society. The rebel stands with a few like him on the outside looking in. What a price to pay for having one's own way!

The Leadership of God

When God's children submit themselves completely to His will and set the Lord Jesus on His throne in their hearts, the problems of submission melt away. When we truly realize that He knows it all and His way is completely right, then we trust our soul to a perfect leadership. God sets a hedge around us. Oh, the security of following the Shepherd of our souls, who leads us beside the still waters!

We *learn* to submit to God. We learn the values of sensitive submission, not blind submission. We cease being the billy-goat, butting into everything in our way, and we become the beloved sheep that are known to Him by name. As we follow our protector, we become like Him; that is the name of the game.

Jesus came into the world, God in the flesh, and showed us what submission is all about. Over and over He tells us that He came to do His Father's will, not His own. He told us that even the words He used were God-picked.

In the garden before His terrible death when He prayed for the cup to pass, if possible, He said, "Not my will by Thine be done." Though He was the Son of God He submitted, lovingly, to humiliation, torture, injustice, reviling, and finally death.

> In the days of His flesh, when He offered up both prayers and supplications with loud crying and tears to the One able to save Him from death, and He was heard because of His piety. Although He was a Son, He learned obedience from the things which He suffered. And having been made perfect, He became to all those who obey Him the source of eternal salvation.
>
> (Hebrews 5:7-9)

Angels and men have dared to disobey their Maker. God chose not to make us robots, but gave us the choice of submission or rebellion. Christ chose to serve God no matter what it cost, and though it cost Him His life, look what it paid Him! He now sits at the right hand of God reigning over the church, His kingdom. He knows that His sensitive submission opened a way to God for us that would have been inaccessible had He refused to die. Does He think the price was too much? No. Was His submission necessary? Yes. Could He have refused? Oh, yes.

> I am the good shepherd; the good shepherd lays down His life for the sheep. . . and I lay down My life for the sheep. . .For this reason the Father loves Me because I lay down My life that I may take it again. No one has taken it away from Me, but I lay it down on My own initiative. I have authority to lay it down, and I have authority to take it up again. This commandment I received from My Father.
>
> (John 10:11,15-18)

Jesus teaches us a lot in this paragraph. God loved Him for His submissiveness. This shows us that God will love us, too, for submissiveness. I want His love. I *need* His love. God gave His Son some rights in this great submissive act. "I have authority to take it up again." We, too, have rights in our submission. Christ chose submission and knew the benefits were worth it. He gave us this example that we, too, should benefit from chosen submission.

Jesus knew that God is not a God of whims and foolishness. The submission that He required is for our good and the good of others. This submission will not make us less a person but a better person. God is busily fitting us for heaven, and humility and sensitive submission are definite characteristics of those who will be utterly saved, "saved to the uttermost" (Hebrews 7:25 KJ).

The apostles were chosen men; they were chosen to be submissive disciples. Eleven of them *were* to the end! One chose another way and went to his own place. One chose not to submit but to have his own way. Where are the eleven now? Would they tell you that submission to Jesus was worthwhile though it cost them their lives? You know they would!

The Lord calls us to follow Him and chooses us to be the elect when we elect to be submissive to Him. Not all choose to submit to the end. We, too, can exchange our crown for something worth less and worthless. Judas loved the money bag and pilfered from it daily. There may be something we love too much in the "bag" we carry while daily worshipping its contents. Oh, the stacks of bags, some of money, or pride, or lusts, or *whatever. . . .*

Submission Required of All Christians to One Another

God spells out to the Christian that submission is a constant daily requirement. His plan is for His child to become a new creature, one like His Father and His Older Brother. God is working with us to cut loose the umbilical cord of our natural, sinful nature and weld us into the silver cord of eternal life. He is preparing for us a prepared place and the one way is the giving up of our own will. It is straight (difficult) and narrow and few seek it.

> Broad is the way that leads to death,
> And thousands walk together there;
> But wisdom shows a narrower path,
> With here and there a traveler.　　(Anon)

"Or do you think that the Scripture speaks to no purpose; 'He jealously desires the Spirit which He has made to dwell in us'? But He gives a greater grace. Therefore it says, 'God is opposed to the proud, but gives grace to the humble.' Submit therefore to God. Resist the devil and he will flee from you" (James 4:5-7).

If we are submitting to His authority and teachings, we are drawing near to God and to our fellow Christians. If we are submitting to Satan and his authority, we are in the process of being lost. When we despise authority we are on the top of the list of the unrighteous. "Then the Lord knows how to rescue the godly from temptation, and to keep the unrighteous under punishment for the day of judgement, and *especially those* who indulge the flesh in its corrupt desires and *despise authority*. Daring, self-willed, they do not tremble when they revile angelic majesties" (2 Peter 2:9,10).

Those who keep peace in the body of Christ serve God and each other. They esteem others better than themselves. This is beautifully accounted in 1 Peter 3:8,9. "To sum up, let all be harmonious, sympathetic, brotherly, kindhearted, and humble in spirit; not returning evil for evil, or insult for insult, but giving a blessing instead; for you were called for the very purpose that you might inherit a blessing."

Another such instruction is given in Philippians 2:3-8.

Do nothing from selfishness or empty conceit, but with humility of mind let each of you regard one another as more important than himself; do not merely look out for your own personal interests, but also for the interests of others. Have this attitude in yourselves which was also in Christ Jesus, who, although He existed in the form of God, did not regard equality with God a thing to be grasped, but emptied Himself, taking the form of a bond-servant, and being made in the likeness of men. And being found in appearance as a man, He humbled Himself by becoming obedient to the point of death, even death on a cross.

Rewards of Submission

As we just noted from the scripture above, God greatly rewarded Jesus for His humility, for His submission. God rewarded Him for His attitude. He praised Jesus because He did not grasp what was rightly His, but gave it up for the better good.

It takes a lot of faith to really believe that God is seeing our submissions; that He is seeing the things done in secret for His name. It is hard to realize that He knows our humiliations and our petty sacrifices, *but He does.*

Someone asked the question, "Can your pride suffer humiliation for the Lord?" Jesus suffered humiliation. The King allowed Himself to be spat on by the lowest of mankind. Those creatures are long gone, but Jesus still rules in honor and majesty two thousand years later.

God promises that He will give grace to the humble. God gives more presents to those who are submissive. His ears are open to the prayers of the righteous. "For the eyes of the Lord are upon the righteous, and His ears attend to their prayer, but the face of the Lord is against those who do evil" (1 Peter 3:12).

It is through submission (obedience to His will) that we gradually form the divine nature and receive the fruits, the likenesses of the Holy Spirit: love, joy, peace, patience, kindness, goodness, faithfulness, gentleness, and self-control. What more could we ask in this life than to take on these marks of Christianity? What better gifts could we seek?

He even exalts the submissive at the proper time. "All of you, clothe yourselves with humility toward one another, for God is opposed to the proud, but gives grace to the humble. Humble yourselves, therefore, under the mighty hand of God, that He may exalt you at the proper time" (1 Peter 5:5,6).

God continues to turn things upside down. His grace runs over to the submissive person, but He shuts off the blessings from the proud. Pride still goes before a fall, as Solomon told us so long ago.

The Marriage Relationship

With all of these thoughts in mind, and despite the cries of our "liberated sisters" the bottom line is still submission for the Christian woman.

Heartbreak and defeat are hers if she sets a foolish course. "Every wise woman buildeth her house: but the foolish plucketh it down with her hands" (Proverbs 14:1 KJ).

As I submit to God and my husband, I build my house. If I rebel, I tear it down. If I have a Christian husband, we submit to each other and to God for the good of each other. Submission is God-blessed and rewarded; it works together for our good. If I do not have a Christian husband, I still submit to him in everything that is not contradictory to God's teachings.

When I submit my body to my husband and he submits to me it makes us both happy. It creates love.

> Let the husband fulfill his duty to his wife, and likewise also the wife to her husband. The wife does not have authority over her own body, but the husband does; and likewise also the husband does not have authority over his own body, but the wife does. Stop depriving one another, except by agreement for a time that you may devote yourselves to prayer, and come together again lest Satan tempt you because of your lack of self-control.
>
> (1 Corinthians 7:3-5)

Christ set the example of complete submission by giving up His life to please His Father. No one took it from Him. He chose to follow even to death. If we choose to marry, we should give ourselves willingly as a submissive wife, yet we are not slaves, but loving companions, fellow-heirs. We are doing what we *chose* to do; we are continuing to choose sensitive submission. Christ was not the less for His submission, nor are we. We *choose* to be worthy women! We choose to help build a Christ-centered home and to raise godly children. We choose to respect our husbands and to appreciate them. We choose for them to have the final say even when we think they are using bad judgement. We don't say it is easy, but we do see that it is better. (There wasn't anything easy about the cross, but it was better. . .for us.)

God fashioned Eve with His own hands and He gave her to Adam to be loved and protected and appreciated. A good wife is a gift from God. He meant for man, the stronger, the leader, to lead and for the woman to follow his lead. Both are happier when it is this way. If a man will not please God in this relationship, will not be submissive to God's instructions concerning his wife, then that man will have to answer to His Head, Christ. "But I want you to understand that Christ is the head of every man, and the man is the head of a woman, and God is the head of Christ" (1 Corinthians 11:3).

God instructs His women to be not only submissive, chaste, respectful, and to emphasize the inward adorning, but also to not be "frightened by any fear" (1 Peter 3:6). Why not be frightened of the physically stronger man? Because God takes care of the one who is "precious in His sight." God will fight her battles. I believe that!

131

If men become God's men and are truly submissive to Him, then the wife's submission becomes a blessing indeed. It is not hard to follow a man who loves you so much that he would die for you (Ephesians 5:25). It is not hard to follow the things that make for peace when you are married to a peacemaker. It is not hard to revere a respected man who reverences God and fears Him. Of course, this is the ideal.

God, in His wisdom, delegates who gives the final word. The final word may not always be the wisest word. Principals, presidents, and papas are not always right, but most of them *try* to be.

God gives a special blessing to the ladies who submit to Him and to their husbands whole-heartedly, for they will be called precious in His sight. *Only through sensitive submission do we develop the imperishable quality of a gentle and quiet spirit. Only* through submission.

Christ was submissive to a cruel Roman band of soldiers. Paul was submissive to the sword of the same government. Peter, tradition says, was crucified head down, as he felt unworthy to die as His Lord. What's so hard about our being submissive to a husband for a little while, even a lifetime?

"But I want you to understand that Christ is the head of every man and the man is the head of the woman and God is the head of Christ" (1 Corinthians 11:3).

Dear Friend,

I just had to send a note to tell you how much I love you and care about you. I saw you yesterday as you were walking with your friends. I waited all day hoping you would want to talk with me also. As evening drew near, I gave you a sunset to close your day and a cool breeze to rest you. And I waited. But you never came. It hurt me, but I still love you because I am your friend.

I saw you fall asleep last night and I longed to touch your brow. So, I spilled moonlight on your pillow and your face. Again I waited, wanting to rush down so that we could talk. I have so many gifts for you. But you awakened late the next day and rushed off to work. My tears were in the rain.

Today you looked so sad, so all alone. It makes my heart ache because I understand. My friends let me down and hurt me so many times, too. But I love you. Oh, if you would only listen to me. I really love you. I try to tell you in the blue sky and in the quiet green grass.

I whisper it in the leaves on the trees and breathe it in the colors of the flowers. I shout it to you in the mountain streams and give the birds love songs to sing. I clothe you with warm sunshine and perfume the air with nature's scents. My love for you is deeper than the oceans and bigger than the biggest want or need in your heart.

If you only knew how much I want to help you. I want you to meet my Father. He wants to help you, too. My Father is that way, you know. Just call me, ask me, talk with me. Please, please don't forget me. I have so much to share with you. But I won't hassle you any further. You are free to call me anytime. It's up to you. I'll wait because *I love you!!*

Your Friend,
JESUS
(Anon.)

Chapter 19

WHOM GOD HAS JOINED TOGETHER

Most little girls dream of their wedding day, even at a tender age. Their imagination can visualize the white gown, the audience, the flowers and the excitement of that never-to-be-forgotten occasion!

I remember one of our little girls after seeing "Bride and Groom" on television, often walking around with a tea towel over her head, kissing the door-post, and saying "I do."

God is very involved in drawing His children together in holy matrimony. His teaching is constant and fervent on marrying wisely.

"Furthermore, you shall not intermarry with them; you shall not give your daughters to their sons, nor shall you take their daughters for your son. For they will turn your sons away from following Me to serve other gods; then the anger of the Lord will be kindled against you, and He will quickly destroy you" (Deuteronomy 7:3,4). Here God lays down the law and the principles of the law on whom to marry and not marry and why. No intermarriage with the God-hater, for they likely would be the stronger and unfaithfulness to God would be the result. We look around us today and see when this principle is violated how tragedy often results for more than one generation.

The new law repeats this instruction in 2 Corinthians 6:14. "Do not be bound together with unbelievers; for what partnership have righteousness and lawlessness, or what fellowship has light with darkness?"

God is telling us that we will not have enough in common with the unbeliever. I think it is interesting that the "unequal yoke" (KJ) or "mismated" (RSV) used in the context of "bound together" (NAS) refer back to the yoke described in Deuteronomy 22:10, "You shall not plow with an ox and a donkey together."

Hopefully, the Christian is the ox, and is plodding along the road of righteousness while the donkey, the non-Christian, is kicking up his heels, doing a lot of braying and halting the progress of the team. It is a sad truth that the second most important decision of our life is "Whom shall I marry?" and it is made in the "donkey-season", our youth.

We parents hear, "I'm *not* too young to marry, it doesn't matter if I finish my education, I won't marry unless she is beautiful (or he is handsome), if it doesn't work we'll get out of it, I want to be my own boss," etc. etc.

The Jews had something in their careful match-making that we still can have in the church today. But we'll come back to that thought.

Usually, when we think of God and match-making, our minds go first to Isaac and Rebekah. Genesis 24. Sarah is gone and Abraham knows that he cannot live much longer. He intends to do all that he can to see that Isaac has a wonderful marriage like the one he had shared with Sarah.

Abraham was a man of faith and he trusted God to give Isaac the right wife. (We, too, should determine this before our children are born). He calls in his wisest servant, the one he could depend on. Swear to me that you will not take for Isaac's wife a woman from the Canaanites. Swear, you will go to my country, to my family, and get Isaac's wife. (When our children marry out of the Lord, they are not choosing from our country, God's family).

The poor servant has a terrible charge to fulfill. He is to go into a land where he knows no one and bring back *the* girl. He asks if he is fortunate enough to find this girl and she refuses to come back with him, should Isaac go there?

No, God put me here and God gave us this land. If God does not turn up a girl who'll leave home, you are released from your vow. (It would be better for Isaac to stay a bachelor than to be wed to a home-sick girl or a Canaanite).

So, the praying servant follows the plan of his master, for he sets out to a place he has never been, to please his lord. He asks God to do something loving for Abraham. Have the right woman at the right time at the well. Have her not only be willing to give me a drink, but willing to water my thirsty animals.

You know, this was a clever test, for *serving* comes hard! He wants the best for Isaac, a woman who will go the second mile. Not many would have passed this test, then or now).

God brings Rebekah to the well. She was beautiful, she was of the family, and she was virtuous. *God* picked out the best one. She may have been the only one, but it just takes one. Here was a girl who had waited for the right man. She knew what she wanted in life, because when she found out the whole story she was ready to go with the servant. She was able to leave her family, knowing that she would never see them again, and as far as is recorded, she never did.

The servant carefully rehearsed the whole matter. Abraham is a blessed man, spiritually and literally. Isaac was born of a mother and father too old to bear children, a miraculous birth. My master will not allow Isaac to marry an unfit woman, for he has said, "She must be of my father's house and of my relatives." I put God to the test and asked Him to send the one He has chosen to the well and that she would not only give me a drink but would water my camels. Rebekah came to the well and did as I asked. She is of the family. She is God-chosen for my master.

The next morning the servant asked for the decision of the family. The family would no doubt have sat up the night discussing the matter. They seem to have come to the conclusion that this was God's will and that He had intervened in the selection of Rebekah for Isaac. They had one request, that Abraham's servant wait ten days before leaving with her.

Can't you feel the heart-break of the mother? Give me ten days, ten last days to be with my lovely Rebekah. Let us weep together and embrace often and store up ten days of memories to live on for the rest of our lives. Practically, give me ten days to get her things together!

The servant said, no, now, today. They called Rebekah and asked her if she would go with this man. She said, "I will go." I'm glad they asked her! If there were lonely days ahead, and there must have been, she knew that *she* had made the choice. She made the right decision, for she was a part of God's plan for Isaac and for God's family. God hand-picked her and He still picks and brings together those who will wait on Him. Sometimes, even from a "far country".

The rest of the story has to be told, though you know it well. It just "happened" that Isaac wasn't in his tent as Rebekah nears, but is out in the field. He heard bells on the camel's neck. (I imagine that he had been watching that road for some time.) Would the servant be successful? What would she look like? Would she be loveable? Or would he have to live the rest of his life lonely?

Rebekah looked up and saw Isaac and quickly dismounted. (She was a fast-moving lady. We saw that in the camel-watering scene.) She asked of the servant who it was that was coming to meet them. When she found that it was Isaac, she veiled herself. She was not ready to be seen, which was discreet. The servant needed to tell Isaac the whole story before he saw her face. He needed to know that she had been chosen by God for him.

Isaac took her into his mother's little home. This was the tent where she had lived and where her treasures were. This was a place for a woman. She took off her veil and he saw how lovely she was. She became his wife and he loved her. *He loved her!* And Isaac could let his mother go, for Rebekah was his comfort.

God tells us so many details in His Book that make the Book so much more personal. She was beautiful, she covered her face, she met him with both feet on the ground, not perched on a camel. He took her into his mother's tent. He loved her and was comforted. These are "meditating" thoughts.

I am convinced that true love, lasting love, dying-for-each-other love comes after marriage. God knows if two children of His continue to plow together in righteousness they'll learn to love each other. Love is always like love. We love our parents, we love our family, we love our brethren, and in time we love our mates.

All real love is patient, kind, not jealous, not arrogant, does not have to have its own way, forgets wrongs suffered, bears it all, believes it all, keeps on hoping, keeps on enduring, and finally, just does not fail (1 Corinthians 13).

Love is at the top of the ladder of Christian growth, it is not in its fullness at the honeymoon. We learn to love. We learn to love our mates. God asks the older Christian women to help the younger women to love their husbands and their children. "That they may encourage the young women to love their husbands, to love their children" (Titus 2:4).

How blessed is a marriage that God arranges! How blessed when the man learns to lead in love and learns to love his wife enough to die for her! He provides for her, he protects her; what a blessed woman to be the recipient of such riches! What a blessed man who has a wife who has learned to love him back, learned to be a worthy woman, learned to be discreet, learned to never bring him shame, learned to stay at home with the small children if at all possible, and learned to reverence and respect her husband! Her price *is* above rubies!

That's the kind of marriage God has in mind for His own. I am confident, *I know* that He still brings together His faithful children if they will only let Him. Too often a Hagar is chosen rashly when a Sarah was in the mind of God.

Many times His children settle for the lesser mate because of a lack of faith and patience. Many girls say "yes" to a man they know is not right because they fear no one else will ask. This is immaturity and usually pays a terrible price!

Not all should be married. There is a great work and life for the single one who chooses to remain that way.

God instructs the young, formerly married to remarry and stay at home and have a family. "Therefore, I want younger widows to get married, bear children, keep house, and give the enemy no occasion for reproach" (1 Timothy 5:14). He would not instruct them to do what is impossible for them to do. He will help them to find a mate, a suitable husband.

With God, all things are possible, even the finding of a God-chosen husband! *You* may have to teach him. You may have to move. You might have to change your image or your ways. Too many want an Isaac without being a Rebekah!

Chapter 20

THE TWO SHALL BECOME ONE

God started everything right. He made everything full-grown and the seed within it to reproduce. The animal and vegetable and fruit world go on as God made it—but not man.

God made the man first and let him live alone. It was a beautiful world to live in and God put Adam to work taking care of the garden.

God wanted Adam to know that he was alone and lonely before He gave him his mate.

Adam named all the animals as God brought them to him and noticed that for each there was a mate; there was male and female in each species. God was directing Adam's thoughts. Though God and Adam walked together daily, there was no constant companion for Adam.

When the time was right, God brought Eve to Adam. He had fashioned her with His own hands. She had been taken from Adam, taken from his rib, under his heart. When he saw her, he knew what had been missing in Eden.

God did not bring him two or three women, but only one, for He wanted the two to become one. "For this cause a man shall leave his father and his mother, and shall cleave to his wife; and they shall become one flesh" (Genesis 2:24). The two becoming one is a long-time process. It takes a long time, a life time, for two people to become one flesh and heart.

Surely there were times with the first man and woman when they tired of each other. There were times they were bound to be angry with each other and maybe even hated one another occasionally. They had no other choice but to make it, and they made it. Adam had had enough of living alone and welcomed married life. In time, Eve learned that it was better to be the helper than to take the lead. They lived together until death did them part and hopefully, they are still together in a better world.

God meant for there to be only one man and one woman in marriage. That is the easy, simple way, but man complicated it. God said, "One," and man says, "Two or three". God says happiness is one; happiness is leaving and cleaving to the one. The world does not listen to God, but He expects His children who wear His name to listen.

Under the old law the honeymooners got a year-long vacation just to be together and get acquainted, to start a foundation of love that would hopefully last a lifetime. Two people could get to know each other pretty well after three hundred and sixty five days together. (One camping trip with good friends can become an eye opener to both parties!)

The better you know each other, the better you will understand each other. As much as brothers and sisters fight and the length it takes for sibling rivalry to disappear when they have been raised alike helps us to see why it takes a long time for strangers to become one. *Loving is easy, but liking is hard!*

If we are wise wives, we soon learn what doesn't work at our house. "A wise woman buildeth her house, but the foolish plucketh it down with her own hands" (Proverbs 14:1 KJ). Experience quickly teaches us that there are some things that cause anger within him that we do not understand, and he finds the same thing within us.

The marriages that grow are the ones that learn to compromise and not demand their own way. It *is* the attitude, isn't it? It isn't easy—but nothing worthwhile is. Too many want a wedding but not a marriage. Their thinking goes like this, "If it isn't peachy-creamy daily then I will keep looking until I find the ideal."

I remember when I was showing off my engagement ring to a pretty lady. She sighed and said, "If I had worked as hard to keep my first husband as I am working to keep my fourth, I'd still be married to the first." Sad, but true, no doubt.

I am convinced that any two committed Christians who are mentally and physically sound can make a go of their vows. We *can* learn to live with anyone who is honestly and sincerely trying to please God and his mate. It may well be that there are others who would be easier to love, more fun to live with, more attractive to the eye, but in the end it gets down to the grind of just *living* with another human being. It gets down to *character*. It gets down to denying self and following the things that make for peace. "God has called us to peace" (1 Corinthians 7:15).

Marriage is for adults. I heard of a famous beauty who said, "If you have not met your mate by the time you are twenty-five, you are lucky". A lot of truth in that. Kids have to have it *their* way; it takes time to learn to give up your way. It takes time to be weaned from home.

God does not want wives to be put away – or husbands either. In fact He hates it. He calls it treachery. A definition of treachery is "violation of allegiance". It is breaking a lifelong vow or commitment. In Malachi He tells some men who had put away their wives that their sacrifices were not being accepted because of those deeds. They said, "For what reason?" 'Because the Lord has been a witness between you and the wife of your youth, against whom you have dealt treacherously, though she is your companion and your wife by covenant' " (Malachi 2:14).

When two have been married for a long time and the process of being welded together has fused their thoughts and minds, then the parting is so much more cruel. The one who has been put away is so vulnerable. The mold has been broken. There is an open, exposed wound that only God and time can heal. This was not God's plan.

Platonic friendships often start innocently, but too often get out of hand. Job's wisdom shows through when he said, "I have made a covenant with my eyes; how then could I gaze at a virgin?" (Job 31:1). We have to watch that "gazing".

God helps us to know how to become one.

> Let your fountain be blessed, and rejoice in the wife of your youth. As a loving hind and a graceful doe, let her breasts satisfy you at all times; be exhilarated always with her love.
>
> (Proverbs 5:18-19)

You can feel excitement in these words! Rejoice, be exhilarated (ravished – KJ) with her love.

> Enjoy life with the woman you love all the days of your fleeting life which He has given to you under the sun; for this is your reward in life, and in your toil in which you have labored under the sun.
>
> (Ecclesiastes 9:9)

God, in His goodness, has made marriage to the same person better in every way as they grow alike. (The philanderer never finds real fulfillment but only temporary excitement.) Why shouldn't marriage be better in every way as you grow together? You have the same kids, the same friends, have shared the same jokes and the same tragedies, and now you are sharing the same grandchildren!

If the man is to continue to court his wife, she must be "courtable". She'll clean up, dress up, and cuddle up. She'll continue to flirt with her husband. A friend once gave me a definition for love. "Love is noticing." She'll be noticing him. In a crowded room, she'll know where he is. She'll often have a certain look in her eyes that started when they dated and still draws like a magnet.

Late statistics show many older couples are divorcing. The children are gone. The romance has died and two strangers have been living in one home. What could be sadder?

If the two have grown steadily together, the sweetest days of all are at hand! The second honeymoon is here! You have more time to be together with fewer distractions. You have more money now that college bills are paid. You can travel now, and eat out, and dress nicer and sleep later. So many battles have been fought and put away. So much has been learned. The red flags have become tattered and are hardly ever needed.

Young wives still have a lot of learning and experiencing to do. They need to become good "timers". Timing is so important in healthy relationships. Some people seem to have a gift of knowing what to say and when to say it. Others have to cultivate it. God tells us to ask for wisdom and He will give it. And He *will* give it – even in timing.

Many young marriages flounder and even die because of bad timing. Never meet your husband at the door with a list of the day's bad news. He's not ready for it. Wait awhile, greet him with excitement. Two of the sweetest words he'll ever hear are, "Daddy's home!"

Feed him, have dinner almost ready when he walks in the door, if you want a lamb and not a bear. Remember he's been out in the jungle all day for you and the kids and he is probably tired and cross.

I remember a comic years ago making a point on this situation. He said, "You come home tired, you drag in the house and your wife says, 'Do you know what Junior did today?' And you say, 'No, tell me, so that I can hate him.'"

All normal people like to go home to a clean, happy, good-smelling house and be greeted by a clean, happy, good-smelling family.

What makes the two become one, really? What makes two become one in purpose, in thought, in hopes and plans, even in peace and war? *Getting to know each other.* That sounds simple, but it isn't. We all have our facades, our masks. We are afraid to let the guard down. Why? Different reasons for different people.

When we are dating we never run out of words. When we marry, often one or both clams up and the marriage dries up! Talking is the answer, explaining ourselves to the other, whether they approve of us or not. Even fighting is a part of communication and is beneficial *if we fight fair.* Even in talking and fighting, timing is important. There has to be enough time to finish the round. It has to be a quiet time, no company, no crying kids, no food burning, and no one in a hurry.

"I want to talk to you. There's something bothering me. You may think it is silly, it *may be* silly, but I want to talk to you about it. I want you to help me work it out, OK?"

This works at our house. (I'm blessed.) He always listens and never laughs at me. (I'm twice blessed.) He may not agree with me, but he gives me a hearing.

Some men won't. I can hear one of those wives asking what do do if he won't listen. Well, let's have a try at that question. Whatever problem we have, there *is* an answer. We may never know the answer but God does. Sometimes, you have to turn your husband over to God. God wants His children to become one and He will help us to have as good a marriage as is possible. "Now to Him who is able to do exceeding abundantly beyond all that we ask or think, according to the power that works within us" (Ephesians 3:20). He can do more with our problems than we think. We often have to get out of the way and let Him work. Sometimes God has to change the wife before He can get the husband to change.

It might be that our mates will not change or will refuse to. Then He will give us grace to bear it and peace in spite of the non-verbilization or whatever.

I believe we can help men to talk more by learning to listen better. Talk about anything they want to talk about whether it is interesting to you or not. Talk about their childhood, their teachers, their relatives, their pets, their former justices or injustices. You are getting to know them and they are learning to trust you. Meanwhile, God is working with you both because He loves you and He wants you to become one. A happily married couple is getting to be a rare thing in our society, but the kingdom of God should have many such couples!

In the same way, you wives, be submissive to your own husbands so that even if any of them are disobedient to the word, they may be won without a word by the behavior of their wives, as they observe your chaste and respectful behavior. And let not your adornment be merely external—braiding the hair and wearing gold jewelry, or putting on dresses; but let it be the hidden person of the heart, with the imperishable quality of a gentle and quiet spirit, which is precious in the sight of God. For in this way in former times the holy women also, who hoped in God, used to adorn themselves, being submissive to their own husbands. Thus Sarah obeyed Abraham, calling him lord, and you have become her children if you do what is right without being frightened by any fear. You husbands likewise, live with your wives in an understanding way, as with a weaker vessel, since she is a woman; and grant her honor as a fellow heir of the grace of life, so that your prayers may not be hindered. To sum up, let all be harmonious, sympathetic, brotherly, kindhearted, and humble in spirit; not returning evil for evil, or insult for insult, but giving a blessing instead; for you were called for the very purpose that you might inherit a blessing.

(1 Peter 3:1-9)

Here is a lengthy teaching to husbands and wives on how to get along. It starts out telling a Christian wife how to get along with a non-Christian husband. Many women become Christians after they are already married. The answer is to live a life in front of him that shows dedication to God and respect and obedience for her husband.

Then God instructs the Christian man how to live with his wife. First, He says, "Live with her in an understanding way". Many men throw up their hands right there and say it is *impossible* to understand a woman. *God does and He will help men to!* God hears godly women pour out their hearts to Him day after day. God hears them ask Him to help them to have a good marriage. God will answer that prayer and will give wisdom to the man who seeks happiness in his home. He will do it for the man's sake and for the woman's. (*Isn't God good!*)

God says not only to live with her in an understanding way, or "according to knowledge" (KJV), but to remember that *she is a woman*—not a man. She is weaker, she hurts quicker, she give up

146

sooner, her emotions are more easily triggered, she dissolves into tears, and she just does not react like a man. *She never will!* She can't! God doesn't expect her to and He teaches men not to expect it either.

Colossians 3:19 says, "Husbands, love your wives, and do not be embittered against them". I believe that men often get bitter toward women because women are women. Rex Harrison sings, "Why can't a woman act like a man?"

Next, God says to grant her honor as a fellow-heir. Don't put her down because she is different, for she will occupy as much heaven as he does. There will not be a "His and Hers" in heaven, just a "Theirs". There will not be a crown for the man and an apron for the woman.

Then, God gives an added incentive for the Christian man to want to treat his wife as God would have him. He says, "If you don't treat your wife as a fellow-heir, your prayers are going to be hindered". Who wants *that* to happen? He is saying that if a man does not treat his wife right then when he calls for help he will get a busy signal!

This brings us around to the goodness of God again. Thank you, Father, this makes me want to cry, and if I ever heard a female reaction, that is it! It is so comforting to know that You understand me when I can't understand myself, and that You look out for all your daughters. We know that we need your understanding, your intercession, and your love. And we need all these qualities in our husbands, too. We thank you for our being women; help us to be precious in Your sight!

We are thankful for marriage and for Your part in making it better all the time. We are thankful that You have given us lovers, protectors, fathers, and husbands all in the same package.

The two of us together, hand in hand, just as You've planned, walking toward Beulah land.

TWO CONTRACTS

A long time back, we made a pact, a contract.
"Until death do us part", made from the heart.
Children were we, unacquainted with misery,
With watching the breath of our child near death,
Of bills unpaid, and jobs that fade,
And hot words said — better unread.

"A wise woman builds her house," He said to me.
　"But if he cared he'd share the responsibility."
"No, it's his lot to provide the bread," He said.
　"But a woman's work is never done, it lasts from sun to sun!"

"A foolish woman tears up her plans with her very own hands", He replied.
　I'll help you learn, wisdom supply,
And be with you till the day you die.
　Nothing will happen we cannot fight,
If you'll trust in Me, it will all end right.

I'm so glad we have come this far.
　That God has changed me much, made you what you are.
I'm even glad that the sun's sinking fast,
　That this old life is rapidly past.

The pact was good, let's make another.
　"The one who goes first will wait for the other."
This contract says no more pain,
　No showers or no more rain.
No more tears or no broken hearts —
　And no more death or ever to part.

Lea Fowler

THE EVENING

As the sun approaches the distant hills,
I reach for her hand with soft caress,
The spark's still there and it always thrills,
It lingers on like our first kiss.

Our love began in the beauty of spring.
The flower of summer came, oh, so soon.
The bud of love that showers bring,
He opened now a perfect bloom.

As autumn leaves are turning gold,
Nature's rose fades and falls,
Slowly true love's bloom unfolds,
Fadeless now is our love as evening calls.

The summit is in sight - we'll soon be there,
Hand in hand we pause, what a view!
The evening of our love is answered prayer,
Sunset, no it's sunrise, and I'll share it with you.

Our Lord said, "and the two shall become one",
But this is hard to do, so easy to say.
Just a partnership, a union for some,
But for me it is oneness, all the way.

Russell Fowler

I Know He Loves Me

Lea Fowler

To do just as I please brings no ful-fill-ment.

To serve my-self a-lone brings on–ly pain.

But to find His will for me will bring con-tentment,

And to fol-low where He leads will be my gain.

Chorus

I know He loves me be cause He died for me.

I know He cherishes me for I'm His Bride,

Be-cause I choose His lead, glo-ri-fy Him as my Lord,

We'll be to-geth-er on the o- ther side.